Moose

Animal

Series editor: Jonathan Burt

Already published

Moose

Kevin Jackson

REAKTION BOOKS

For Monty

Published by
REAKTION BOOKS LTD
33 Great Sutton Street
London EC1V ODX, UK
www.reaktionbooks.co.uk

First published 2008

Printed and bound in China

British Library Cataloguing in Publication Data
Jackson, Kevin, 1955–
    Moose. – (Animal)
    1. Moose
    I. Title
    599.6'57

ISBN: 978 1 86189 396 3

Contents

Introduction

They are God's own horses . . .
Thoreau, *The Maine Woods* (1864)

.

Moosehead Lake, Maine, a chilly September evening, about a decade ago. My wife Claire and I had travelled in from the coast to join one of the commercial moose watches that are a mainstay of the local tourist economy. The trip had not been a great success. A couple of hours of puttering around on the placid waters in a small motor-boat had yielded no more than a single sighting, and not a very satisfying one at that: in the gathering dusk, a solitary bull moose, off in the distance, just about perceptible through binoculars. It hardly amounted to an epiphany.

Then the boat's motor cut out. Our guide tried to radio back to base for help, but either no one was monitoring his calls or his radio was dead, too. It was all starting to look a bit grim. Maine nights can already be dangerously cold in September, and none of us was wearing proper outdoor gear. Fortunately, one of the other aspiring moose-watchers was a former US Marine with a knack for mechanics. He took the motor to pieces, fiddled with it for a while, and within half an hour or so we were all having cocktails and looking forward to a hot dinner.

So the drive back to our motel was a mixture of relief and disappointment, right up until the moment when I drew Claire's attention to the life-sized statue of a moose on the roadside – we'd noticed it earlier, in full daylight. Slight pause. It slowly dawned on both of us that the statue had been on the other side of the road . . .

We stopped, turned the car round, went cautiously back up the road in first gear. There, a good 6 feet (2 metres) or more tall at the withers and nonchalantly chomping on foliage, was a fully grown cow moose. The species is famously timid, with the exceptions of males during rutting season and mothers with their young, so we were surprised at how little she seemed to care about our presence. We edged the car forward until she was barely 3 or 4 feet from the headlights, turned off the engine, and watched.

Many of those who have written about the moose comment on how comical, even grotesque the beast is – a gift to cartoonists. Their muzzles (one cartoonist irreverently called the moose muzzle a 'schnozzola') have been judged preposterously long, their tails ludicrously short, the humps above their withers Quasimodo-ish, their expressions foolish. Ted Hughes, in a comic poem for children, calls them 'dopes of the deep woods', and many people assume that the poor moose is as stupid as it is bulky.

But this cow moose did not look silly at all. 'Majestic' doesn't hit the right note, since there was nothing overpowering about her largeness. Quite unexpectedly, the feature that enraptured us most was her ears: large, delicate, constantly in nervous motion as she picked up on the many noises of the night-time forest. (Thoreau, I later found out, compared them to a rabbit's ears.) Their sensitivity, their quick movement, seemed expressive of an intense alertness. She was anything but clumsy and sluggish and dumb. She was a beauty.

I have seen plenty of other animals in the wild – dolphins and whales in the Atlantic, porcupines and martens in Italy, wallabies and camels in Australia – but I have never experienced such a sense of privilege and enchantment as I felt watching this peaceable she-creature. After about twenty minutes, she ambled away into the foliage and was gone. In the following days, we saw several more moose at close range, including a frisky youngster cantering down a roadside. But you never forget the first time.

This, then, really was something of an epiphany, and all the more telling for its unexpected timing. But why had I come in search of this particular epiphany? A full answer would, I suspect, not be particularly interesting to anyone but me. Enough for now to say that, some time around the early 1980s, it began to be obvious that, though interested in many species of animal, I was developing a fascination for moose above all other beasts. Were I more of a New Age type, I might perhaps want to make the embarrassing claim that the moose declared itself as my totem animal, my spirit creature, or what have you. Perhaps. All I know is that I was more and more drawn to images and tales and lore of moose.

Friends and colleagues began to call me by the nickname 'Moose'; they still do. For one of my birthdays, I was given an adoption share in a bull moose at a London zoo. (It died soon afterwards, allegedly in mourning for its mate.) When I founded a small poetry imprint in the 1990s, I called it Alces Press – *Alces alces* being the Linnaean term for moose. When the Internet came along, I built the word 'alces' into my email address. I could go on. It never really occurred to me that one day I might tackle my interest in some more systematic way; so the chance to write this small book was another kind of unexpected pleasure.

In a sense, moose do not exist.

Not as distinct species, that is. There is no biological difference between the North American moose and the European elk.

When reports started to filter back from the New World about an extraordinary new quadruped, larger than any known deer and equipped with startling headwear, Europeans grew excited: it sounded like yet another wonder of the lands opened up by Columbus. Some speculated that this so-called 'moose' beast might be the living relative of the notorious Giant Irish Elk, known only from fossil remains. But it was all moose ado about nothing: the American wonder was simply an old world ungulate in a different forest-land.

Why was the mistake possible? Mainly because North America was being colonized by the British, the French and the Spanish – men and women from countries in which the elk had long since been hunted into extinction. A few hundred more Norwegians, Swedes or Russians among the colonists and the mistake might never have happened. Without such Northerners, the blunder was almost inevitable.

It happened like this: since the first settlements, mainly in Virginia, were well to the south of the standard moose ranges, they met with two smaller types of deer. The smaller was the

In some districts moose have become a significant modern traffic hazard, but North American moose still tend to shun built-up areas . . .

. . . while in Norway, moose have become increasingly bold in recent years.

so-called Virginia, or whitetail deer, *Cariacus virginianus*, and this the colonists called simply 'deer'. Seeing that the other type was quite large, and recalling that the European elk was noted for its size, they called this quadruped an 'elk'. In fact, it was not an elk at all, but a wapiti – *Cervus canadiensis*, that is, not *Cervus alces*. So when colonists moved northwards, and first encountered a genuine elk, they were obliged to call on the native terms: *moose* is derived from an Algonquian word. A new linguistic bottle, an old biological wine.

Compared with many of the other species in the Reaktion Animal series – snake, ant, dog, horse – the moose is an elusive beast, and every bit as elusive in cultural history as in the wild. South America has never been home to the moose, or Africa, or the Indian sub-continent, or most of China (Manchuria is the exception), or Australia, or – as noted – large parts of Western Europe, for the past couple of thousand years. Homer, Dante, Cervantes, Shakespeare and Camoens have nothing to say of

The logo for Moosehead, a leading Canadian beer brand.

the beast; Giotto, Michelangelo and Rembrandt never painted it. (Though the German-born artist Carl Rungius did become known as 'the Rembrandt of the Moose'.) Hunt for the moose through library indexes and stacks and, nine times out of ten, he will escape you. Then, finally, he will turn up where you might least expect him – in the castle of the Danish astronomer Tycho Brahe, for example, where you will find him drinking large quantities of beer.

Despite his existence on the margins of human life, the moose has ambled into some major historical events and encountered

A Snowdonia Ale moose logo'd pump clip, from the Welsh brewery Purple Moose.

some exceptional characters. His story includes Julius Caesar – the first writer ever to note down the existence of 'Alces' – and two of America's greatest presidents, Thomas Jefferson and Theodore Roosevelt. (Benjamin Franklin also puts in a cameo appearance.) Albrecht Dürer painted a moose, and later put him in the Garden of Eden; George Stubbs, greatest of all equine portraitists, also limned one of the first moose ever seen in England. Some of America's leading nineteenth-century men of letters – James Russell Lowell, Henry David Thoreau – went on moose hunts, and left eloquent records of their findings.

The spread of Christianity across Canada by Jesuit missionaries was fuelled almost exclusively by moose meat, as was the secular empire of the Hudson's Bay Company, which at one time had dominion over one-twelfth of the planet's land surface. Many Native American tribes subsisted almost wholly on moose flesh, and a few remote peoples of Northern regions have carried that dependence into the twenty-first century. Moose imagery thrives in heraldry and animation, branding and comic strips, and at least one cartoon moose has inspired critical studies of his own: the incomparable Bullwinkle, of *Rocky and Bullwinkle* fame.

The moose has become, variously, an emblem of the North (Sweden and Norway have both adopted the moose as their official animal; Canadian companies, such as Moosehead Beer, also exploit these northerly associations); of the endangered or enduring wilderness; of righteous wrath (many military units have worn moose insignia); or, in the case of the international organization of Moose Lodges, of integrity and consideration for others. These are quite heavy burdens of significance even for a creature as large, sturdy and tractable as a moose. The following chapters will attempt to cast some light on the ways in which they came into being.

1 The Natural Moose

The largest living member of the deer family Cervidae, moose are natives of the higher northern hemisphere, and particularly of its mountain tundra regions and boreal forest-lands. These spread from Alaska down through Canada and into some northern parts of the United States; and then from Scandinavia, across the northern Eurasian continent into Siberia and northern parts of China.

Depending on its sub-species and gender, the adult moose will weigh something in the regions of 550–770 lb (1,210–1,694 kg) (for *Alces alces cameloides,* or Manchurian moose, the smallest) to 880–1,540 lb (1,936–3,388 kg) (*A. alces gigas,* or Alaskan moose, the largest), though the Kenai Moose Research Center in Soldotna, Alaska, once kept a bull moose that reached 1,699 lb (3,738 kg). Generally speaking, moose decrease in size the further south they live. Their height at the shoulders is usually in the range of 65 to 79 inches (165 to 200 cm) for bulls and 62 to 69 in. (157 to 175 cm) for cows, while the body length varies from 91 to 113 in. (231 to 287 cm) in bulls and 87 to 111 in. (221 to 282 cm) in cows.

The species' most famous feature is, of course, the large set of antlers worn by adult bull moose.[1] Unlike the antlers of any other deer, moose antlers are broad and flat – the exact term is 'palmate' – with points, or 'tines', along the outer edge. When the

bull moose is standing upright and alert, they look somewhat like a pair of giant hands, opened up with the palms facing the sky. The average length of a single antler is from about 27 in. (68 cm) at the narrower end of the range to 39 in. (99 cm) at the broader. The main function of antlers is sexual attraction – cows favour bulls with big antlers – though they are also used in ritual dominance displays, sparring and actual combat with other males. Antlers are grown and shed on an annual basis, controlled by secretions of testosterone, and bulls from five to

An Alaskan bull moose displays its massive antlers. Recent scientific studies appear to prove that antlers may significantly improve the animal's hearing.

twelve years old usually have the most impressive racks. Bulls shed their antlers, quickly and more or less symmetrically, some time between mid-December and the end of January; if they are impatient to shed, they may well thump them against trees.

New antlers begin to grow at once, and rapidly, fed by blood vessels in the skin, which is covered with a soft, velvet-like covering of short hairs. Full growth takes about 90 to 140 days, with full growth usually being achieved by late August; in early September the bulls rub their antlers vigorously against shrubs and trees, stripping away the velvet and, usually, eating it. Once fully exposed, the antlers are ready to play their part in courtship and related activities. Bulls will now begin to take part in dominance displays – more or less ritual sparring matches, rather than actual fights, between males who have already established some patterns of dominance and subordination. The sparring pair will carefully lower their heads, lock antlers and twist their necks until one submits and rapidly backs

A European elk with antlers in velvet, painted by Priscilla Barrett.

off to avoid injury. Such strenuous engagements may last as long as an hour. In rare instances, when the antlers become permanently locked, the competing pair will be stuck together until they both die of exhaustion or starvation.

Among the other highly distinctive features of moose is a large flap of skin, known as a 'dewlap' (or sometimes 'bell'), which dangles down from the chin like a beard. Small to barely noticeable on calves and cows, and sometimes missing from older bulls after having been frozen away in harsh winters, the dewlap is a mysterious development whose precise function remains debatable, though it is possible that it plays some role in protecting the animal from heat stress: moose feel over-heated when temperatures rise above 23°F (-5°C) in winter or above 57°F (14°C) in summer – which is why the animals never migrated to the southern parts of the United States or to continental Europe. The dewlap is crammed with blood vessels, in which blood may be rapidly cooled by close proximity to the air before returning to the inner furnace of the moose's central frame.

A third highly idiosyncratic feature is the moose's gigantic muzzle – which can easily grow to 20 inches and more, and which ends with that combination of prominent rounded nose and pendulous upper lip traditionally known to Anglophone connoisseurs of moose-meat as 'the muffle' (considered a great delicacy among Native Americans for countless generations). Moose have a highly sensitive naso-labial development on their muffles that appears to help them judge the quality of twigs and leaves. The inner surface area of a moose's nasal cavities holds millions of scent receptors – about 200 times as many as humans possess.

Finally, moose may quickly be identified by a conspicuous hump at the shoulders. This is created by the elongated vertical

'The True Moose or Elk', from L. J. Fitzinger's popular natural history of mammals, *Wissenschaftlich-Populäre Naturgeschichte . . .* (1860).

spines – dorsal processes – of the shoulder vertebrae, which, together with highly developed shoulder muscles, help support the creature's weighty head and antlers.

Moose possess two layers of hair. Their primary, and highly effective, insulation from cold comes from a dense layer of grey fur, made up of hairs that are about an inch in length, which covers the entire body except for the legs and face. Over this layer lies a layer of longer hairs, usually dark brown, varying in length from about 4 to 10 in. (11 to 26 cm). Thus, the usual colouration for an adult moose will be predominantly dark brown, with a grey belly and white lower legs. Younger moose calves tend to be much lighter in colour – red to reddish brown over most of the body, with some grey or black on the legs and belly, and also on the muzzle, ears, shoulders, neck and chest – but grow a darker, grey-brown coat at about two to three months. As yearlings, they are still lighter and greyer than their seniors; they do not grow an adult coat until their second year.

For the first five weeks of their lives, moose calves are vulnerable to almost any predator.

Variations on this basic colour pattern are due to conditions including habitat and the breeding cycle. Eurasian moose, and those of the eastern parts of North America, are often darker than their relatives in the northern and western territories, while Alaskan moose are distinguished by a lighter colouring along their backs, save for a strip of near-black hair running along the spine from the shoulder hump backwards. There have been occasional sightings of white moose in Alaska and Canada. During the mating season, sex hormones bring changes to the facial colouration of Northern European moose: bulls take on very dark brown to black faces, while females become lighter brown. Both sexes of European moose, however, tend to have dark faces.

An annual moult begins in the late winter and early spring on the shoulder hump, before spreading backwards over the rest of the body and forwards along the sides of the neck towards the ears. A new winter coat grows up over the course of the summer and is complete by late September.

LIFE CYCLE

After a gestation period of some 231 days, moose calves are born in the course of a two-week period starting in the middle of May (southern regions) to the end of May (northern regions). The calf weighs something between 22 and 35 lb (48.4 and 77 kg), and the ratio of males to females is equal. Contrary to the reports of early settlers in the New World, who said that cows usually produced at least three 'fawns' each year, it is not common for cows to give birth to more than one or two calves; twins will be much more common in high-quality habitats with ample food supplies and relatively low moose population densities. The usual sites for calving will be secluded areas with heavy

A moose calf, from a promotional card given away in tea packets, c. early 1960s.

ground cover, and easy escape routes from predators. The cow will choose a new calving site each year, at least a mile or so distant from the previous location.

A moose calf can stand on its own four legs within two days of being born and swim within seven. By the age of five weeks, calves are swift enough to escape from the slower forms of predators, such as bears, but they continue to rely on their mothers for protection over the first three seasons of their life, and will rarely wander more than 150 feet (45 m) from their sides. The close rapport between cow and calf comes to an abrupt and, for the calf, bewildering end the following April, about two weeks before the mother is about to give birth again. If the yearling cannot be persuaded to separate by diplomatic means, the mother may resort to violence, until the spurned yearling wanders off either into solitude or the company of other newly rejected offspring.

During their first three years, young bulls and cows grow at about the same rate. Then the cow's growth rate declines, until she reaches her maximum size at the age of five. Bulls continue to grow for another two, three or four years, until they are about 30 to 40 per cent larger than the females. Both sexes live until an average age of sixteen to eighteen, though in rare instances a moose may survive into its early twenties.

In the course of a typical year, the body weight of an adult moose will vary by some 20 to 55 per cent, these changes being

The rapport between a mother and her calf is essential to the species' survival.

primarily a function of the breeding cycle, though the amount and quality of available food obviously plays its part. A bull moose reaches its maximum annual body weight just before the breeding season, or rut. During the rut he will lose all interest in food, and shed as much as 20 per cent of his body weight in eighteen days. When the rut is over, he will then try to rebuild his body by eating as much as possible, but this attempted feast always coincides with the onset of winter, and he may continue to lose another 10 to 25 per cent of his weight. Cow moose reach their maximum weight in early winter, then lose about 10 to 15 per cent of it before the coming of spring.

Most moose, whether bulls or cows, do not become reproductively active until they are some two and a half years old. Bulls are at their reproductive peak between the ages of five and ten; cows between four and twelve. Both sexes look their best in the breeding season that begins in September, the bulls with full-sized antlers and the cows with glossy coats. Males put the majority of effort into courtship, though the precise nature of their work depends on terrain.

In tundra regions, bulls will begin by marking out territory and defending it from competitors, and then dig rutting pits, in which they urinate and wallow, so as to cover themselves with the attractive smell of male hormones – a smell that also accelerates ovulation in the female. Immature bulls will sometimes try to fake their way to sexual intercourse by jumping in an older moose's pit, though the latter will usually thwart the attempt. Drawn by this scent, cows – as many as five to ten at a time – will gravitate towards the pit and wait for the bull's attentions, sometimes fighting amongst themselves for precedence.

In forests, bulls will announce their presence by thrashing trees with their antlers, calling and urinating, often covering several miles in a day. Cows also call to announce their readiness to mate, usually on shorelines or in other places where sound will carry a fair distance. Since more than one bull will respond to a cow's call, fights are common, though most moose will soon retreat at the sight of a bull with a much larger rack. When neither party backs down, the clash will be violent, and the loser may be so badly gored that he will either die from infection or soon be brought down by predators.

Like their tundra brothers, forest bulls will also dig and perfume rutting pits. (They can detect oestrus in the cow by 'flehmen', a scenting action also found in the domestic cat and other mammals, which involves curling back the upper lip and sucking the scented air back towards a specialized set of nasal receptors.) Copulation itself lasts a scant five seconds; the bull may move on as little as ten minutes later, and immediately try to find another cow. A successful bull may breed as many as twenty times in the course of a rut.

DIET, HABITAT AND RANGE

Moose are herbivores, and subsist mainly on twigs in the winter months and aquatic vegetation (which is why they are so often found in or near ponds, lakes and slow-moving streams), shrubs, deciduous trees, and herbaceous plants in the summer – months in which they may spend as many as ten hours a day eating to build up their body stores against the coming winter, and will consume some 45 to 50 pounds of high-quality vegetable matter every day. Though they have been known to feed on several hundred different plant species, their three main staples are aspen, birch and willow, supplemented by many other different types of tree. Hence their principal habitat is boreal forest-land, particularly those forests dense with spruce, fir, aspen, poplar and birch. They can also be found in river delta

A 'Wyoming' or 'Yellowstone' moose in typical feeding mode, in Yellowstone Park, Wyoming.

systems, shrub tundra, coastal forests and the like – anywhere, in fact, where fire, storm, wind and other kinds of massive disturbance churns up the rich mineral nutrients that are taken in by their favoured plants.

Like cows, moose are ruminants, with a four-chambered stomach which enables them to regurgitate partially digested food for dental grinding – chewing the cud. Food is fermented in the first stomach, the rumen, and its nutrients extracted by the next three. During the summer, they will typically eat for one or two hours and then lie down to ruminate, favouring the cooler hours of dawn, dusk and night-time for feeding, since they are highly sensitive to heat stress. It used to be believed that moose used aquatic feeding as a way to stay cool, but this seems to be disproved by the fact that they usually leave the deeper waters after mid-morning, preferring the shadow of trees (dense, low-lying conifers) and the shallow water and mud of sedge meadows and bogs. Their sensitivity to heat can hold long-term hazards, since in extended periods of hot weather they will choose to spend their time staying cool rather than eating, and so may not store enough energy for the winter.

As the weather cools and the mating season begins, moose move into more open areas – meadows and the shorelines of lakes and rivers. When the snows start to fall, they move into areas that can supply both browsing and (coniferous) cover – the latter serving both as shelter from the winds and as concealment from predators. As the temperature drops, they become day- rather than night-feeders, and spend fewer and

'A Moose-Yard', from Richard Lydekker's *Royal Natural History* (1894).

fewer hours eating – down to a minimum of about five hours a day on twigs that are older and take longer to digest – and much more time ruminating. As the snows deepen and become more hardened, moose move back from relatively open areas into mature conifer forests, where the snow is shallower and less solidly crusted.

These changes of circumstance and need usually compel a degree of migration, though not of any epic distance – sometimes as little as a few miles, sometimes as much as 60. The home range of a moose – the individual area it needs for sustenance and comfort – remains about the same in summer and winter, though there are distinct geographical variations, and bulls require larger home ranges than cows. Where the Shiras Moose of Wyoming tend to require little more than a square mile or so each, more northerly sub-species demand from 10

An iconic midwinter glimpse of a moose chased by a pack of wolves across Isle Royale, Michigan, in 1973. After 2 miles the moose turned and made a stand.

A cow moose, killed by a wolf pack in 1950s Alaska.

to 15 square miles, while in Alaska a moose may require up to 112 square miles. Though not particularly territorial, they are creatures of routine and will often use the same habitats for several years.

Apart from *homo sapiens* – potentially the most deadly of all their enemies – a wide variety of other mammals also preys on moose. In Eurasia and North America, the main predators are brown and black bear and wolves, though cougars can also be a major threat in some parts of America. Bears pose a particular danger to moose calves, and in some areas may kill as much as 50 per cent of the new generation, compared to a maximum predation rate of some 20 per cent by wolves. Bears will seldom try to attack an adult moose unless it is old, injured or ailing. Wolves, too, prey on grown moose with great wariness, since a single well-aimed blow from a moose's hoof can kill or fatally injure. On the whole, packs of wolves will attempt to bring down an adult moose only if it shows some signs of weakness.

The other great threat to moose populations is the parasite. They are susceptible to about twenty types of internal parasite – including a nematode worm that lodges in the membranes of the brain and spinal cord, and causes so-called moose sickness, of which the symptoms include blindness, partial paralysis, disorientation and eventual collapse – and several external parasites, notably the 'moose tick', which causes blood loss, hair loss, inflammation and itching so severe that a moose will expend dangerous amounts of winter energy in grooming or rubbing against trees. A bad outbreak of ticks can kill off 20 to 25 per cent of a given moose population over a single winter.

CLASSIFICATION

Linnaeus called the Moose *Cervus alces*, *Cervus* being 'deer' and *alces* 'elk'. But because of an unfortunate confusion with the so-called North American elk, or wapiti (*C. elaphus*) – see the Introduction for a fuller account of this category error – the moose was later given its own genus of *Alces* and reclassified as *A. alces*.

The fossil record for moose is patchy, sometimes almost inexplicably so: for example, there is no known fossil record for moose in north-western Alaska during the Upper Pleistocene, a period when many other large mammals, including mammoths and bear, were crossing over from the Eurasian land mass. Though the broad lines of development and migration are clear enough, there are enough gaps to leave room for conjecture.

ANCESTORS

Mammals first appeared on the world stage some 70 million years ago. The earliest known ancestors of all ruminant quadrupeds were established in both North America and Europe about 40 million years ago; these included the so-called 'pseudodeer' (*Merycodontinae*) of North America, which possessed antler-like growths of live bone from their heads; unlike true antlers, these were neither cast nor regrown.

All known forms of deer, living and extinct, appear to have evolved from protodeer – *Dicrocerideae*. These gave way to the modern *Cervidae*, which includes deer, wapiti and caribou; the members of this genus all have deciduous antlers (save for two genera, the water deer, *Hydropotes*, and the musk deer, *Moschus*). The earliest members of *Cervidae* appeared some 20 million years ago – the early Miocene – in Eurasia. Some of these creatures and their descendants eventually migrated to Europe and the Americas.

It was during the late to middle Pleistocene, some two million years ago, that the immediate forebears of *Alces* evolved, becoming larger in the body but shorter in the neck, with expanded vertebrae; their dentition changed from hypsodont (high crown) to brachydont (low crown), but they retained long nasal bones. The earliest true ancestor of the moose – *Libralces gallicus* (also known as *A. gallicus*) or Gallic moose – evolved in the savannahs of Western Europe some two million years ago. During the late to middle Pleistocene, it eventually spread as far north as the British Isles. Smaller than other broad-fronted moose, it appears to have been suited to long-distance running, and its antlers, which grew to about 10 feet (3 m), had small semicircular palms and tines; it looked more like a modern deer than a moose.

Other, more recent ancestors included the much larger Broad-fronted moose or *L. latifrons* (also *A. latifrons*), which developed around 900,000 to 700,000 BC. As its English name suggests, this creature had a skull that was both broader and higher than today's moose. These creatures grew to a maximum body size – as much as 3,000 lb (136 kg) – during the glacial Pleistocene. Though still quite deer-like in certain respects, *L.*

latifrons bore a number of obvious similarities to the moose, with more or less symmetrical antlers growing up to 8.5 feet (2.6 m). The late Pleistocene also saw the origins of the giant stag moose, *Cervalces scotti*, which had massive tri-palmated antlers that grew laterally out from the skull, much as in the moose. It is possible that this creature was a transitional stage between *Libralces* and *Alces*; it became extinct towards the end of the Holocene, *circa* 9,000 BC.

All North American moose originated in Siberia. It was about a quarter of a million years ago that *L. latifrons* crossed the so-called Bering Land Bridge between what is now the Chukchi Peninsula in Siberia and the Seward Peninsula in Alaska. This ground link between the continents, now the Bering Strait, has opened and been re-flooded at least four times over the last two million years; by the time of the wisconsin glaciation, about 75,000 years ago, the Broad-fronted Moose was extinct and the modern moose was established as a New World creature.

Petroglyph of a moose, from prehistoric Russia.

SUB-SPECIES

Biologists have identified at least eight sub-species of *A. alces* – one, the Caucasian moose (*A. alces caucasicus*) having been hunted into extinction by the early nineteenth century – distinctions between each type being based mainly on variations in size and proportion.

Of the survivors:

Old World

The Siberian Moose (*A. alces pfizenmayeri*) can be found in the northern territories of the former Soviet Union. (Soviet scientists once proposed that this sub-species should itself

Moose God (after Goya), an ink drawing by Magnus Irvin: memory of ancient tribal worship?

Joseph Wolf, watercolour of an elk, c. 1850; Wolf probably studied the elk at the Earl of Derby's famous menagerie at Knowsley, near Liverpool.

An elk bred at the Knowsley menagerie, from an 1851 copy of the *Illustrated London News*.

be divided into the small Western Siberian moose, *A. alces pfizenmayeri*, and the larger Eastern Siberian moose, *A. alces buturlini*, but the suggested distinction has not found much support.)

The European Moose (*A. alces alces*) inhabits some easterly and northerly parts of Europe (very sparsely), western Russia and Scandinavia.

The Manchurian Moose (*A. alces cameloides*) lives in south-east Siberia, northern China and north-east Mongolia.

New World

The Alaskan or Tundra Moose (*A. alces gigas*) lives in Alaska, the Yukon and north-western British Columbia.

The Shiras Moose (also known as the Yellowstone or Wyoming Moose: *A. alces shirasi*) can be found in the southern parts of British Columbia and Alberta, as well as Washington, Idaho, Utah, Montana, Wyoming and Colorado.

The Northwestern Moose (*A. alces andersoni*) is a native of north-western Ontario, Manitoba, Saskatchewan, Alberta, British Columbia, the Northwest Territories and the Yukon territory, as well as North Dakota, Minnesota, Wisconsin and Michigan.

The Eastern or Taiga Moose (*A. alces americana*) is resident in New York, New Hampshire, Vermont, Massachusetts, Maine, New Brunswick, Nova Scotia, Quebec and Ontario. (*Taiga* is the adopted name in North America for the forested area around the Great Lakes, the range in which these moose arrived and from which they spread.)

Towards the end of the nineteenth century, it seemed likely to many anxious naturalists that some if not all of these subspecies would go the way of the unfortunate Caucasian moose, and would be hunted into extinction. This grim tale, and its unexpectedly bright outcome, is one of the main themes of the following chapters, which tell the history of moose and man.

2 The European Moose or Elk

Here's my wisdom for your use,
    as I learned it where the moose
And the reindeer roared where Paris roars tonight . . .
Rudyard Kipling

Migrating from the same ancestral homestead – probably in
eastern Siberia – thousands of years ago, the elk of Europe
journeyed westward, while his brother, the moose, turning
toward the rising sun, crossed over to the North American
continent.
Samuel Merrill, *The Moose Book*

What drove their westward migration? The usual forces:
increasing density of population, decreasing resources of food,
water and other essentials. As the forests of northern Siberia
dwindled, the elk (*Cervus alces*) spread out across the plains of
European Russia, and eventually roamed as far as the Atlantic
coast. At one point, most of central and western Europe, including the southern slope of the Pyrenees and the Alps, became its
home territory.

But as competition with other species, especially *Homo
sapiens*, grew more intense, the migrant elk drew back once
more to the far north and the east – Scandinavia, Russia –
where they remain to the present day. Moose/elk became rare
in France during the fifth and sixth centuries AD, and had van-
ished entirely there by the tenth century. In Switzerland they
died out some time during the Middle Ages. They also became
all but extinct in southern Germany by the ninth century,
though there are records of legal prohibitions against elk
hunting in certain territories near the lower Rhine as late as
1025, which seems sound evidence that in some regions they

may have survived for quite a while longer.

In northern Germany they persisted for several centuries. According to records of game hunting in Brandenburg, in the period from 1612 to 1619, one Johann Sigismund killed 11,598 wild animals, of which 112 were elk. Hunting was not the only threat to the elk: disease took its toll, as did the spread of agriculture. Records suggest that the elk became extinct in Saxony in 1746, in Galicia in 1760 and in Silesia in 1776. A fairly large pocket of elk remained in western Prussia until 1830, when complaints that elk were damaging the forests by eating the twigs of saplings prompted a systematic cull.

In eastern Prussia, the elk's fate was happier, at least for a while. The forest of Ibenhorst – near the mouth of the Memel, close to the Russian border – held something in the region of 300 to 400 elk, all protected by legislation. After the Revolution

A 25-rouble Belarusian bank-note, from the author's collection.

of 1848, however, the regulation was briefly lifted, and the local peasants went on a killing spree. Within a single season, only sixteen elk were left alive; and the price of elk meat plunged to five *pfennige* a pound. Protective legislation was reintroduced and the local stock was augmented by the import of some Swedish elk. By the start of the twentieth century, the elk population had grown to about 1,000.

Thanks to the enormous wilderness spaces of Russia, local elk populations were able to withstand drastic culls and continue to thrive there in large numbers to the present day. In Siberia, moose were often used as mounts, until the practice was forcibly curtailed in the sixteenth century by the Cossack leader Yermak Timofeyvich, who was sent to subdue the region by Ivan the Terrible. In the Taiga (the coniferous forests), so it was said, a moose rider could easily outrun Cossacks mounted on horses. Yermak ordered all moose riders to be put to death, and moose taming was banned.

A. Martenson, author of *Der Elch* (Riga, 1903), made a study of reports from the principal fur and hide markets of the Russian empire in the period shortly before the Revolution. 'According to returns gathered by N. Turkin and others, the number of skins of wild animals taken yearly in Russia amounts to about 50,000,000, of which from 250,000 to 300,000 are elk.' Extrapolating from this kill, Martenson estimated that some two million or more elk lived within the empire's boundaries. Incidentally, one of the islands on which St Petersburg is built, Wassilij-Ostrow, was earlier known by the Finnish name Hirwi-Saari: 'Elk Island'.

It was not only a craving for fresh venison that made the elk such a desirable quarry. Elk hide was greatly favoured as clothing for soldiers, since it was tough enough to withstand crude bullets and other projectiles, but far more flexible than metal armour. King Gustavus Adolphus of Sweden wore a doublet of elk skin for the battle of Lützen in 1632; unfortunately for him, it was not quite strong enough to withstand the enemy bullet that killed him just as he saw victory. And Paul I, Tsar of Russia, was so persuaded of the virtues of elk skin that he ordered that all his cavalry should be issued with hide breeches. To meet this need, thousands of elks died, and it was said that the near-extinction of elk in Poland was a direct result of this order.

Civilians, too, found many uses for the skin and other products of the dead elk. Elk-skin jackets were greatly prized by traders; the skin also made gun sheaths, various types of pouch and wallet, and – in the Middle Ages – slings for hurling stones. Upholsterers made domestic cushions and saddle paddings from elk skin, often using the hair as filling. Antlers provided, whole, the decorations for hunting lodges and grand houses, and, cut up, the materials for knife handles and countless other utensils. Glue for cabinetmaking could be extracted from the unused antler fragments. Medical wisdom of the day attributed curative properties to the left hind hoof of the elk (see below), and the other three hooves could be carved into combs, cups and table furniture. The most humble residue of the dead beast, fat, could be used to produce first-rate candles.

Sometimes, the elk was destroyed simply for being a pest. The ancient laws of West Gotland – in the southern part of modern-day Sweden – classified the elk as a 'noxious animal', comparable to the fox, the wolf, the lynx and the bear, and bounties were offered for elk corpses.

The aristocratic classes of Europe took an entirely different view of the elk from their peasants and merchants, and regarded it chiefly as an enjoyable quarry for their sports. Elk drives were a popular diversion of the nobility and royalty throughout the higher latitudes. In September 1837 King Frederick I of Sweden hosted a drive that lasted a full four days and yielded twelve dead elk, as well as many other mammals. When, as Prince of Wales, Edward VII visited Sweden in 1885, he was treated to an elk drive of vast proportions. According to the popular writer on big game hunting, Sir Henry Pottinger, hundreds of beaters were used in 'sweeping with a gigantic cordon, which was never relaxed by day or night, an enormous extent of forest, and moving the elk gradually to the stations of the guns.' Forty-nine elk perished in a single day.

An Englishwoman, Anne Taplin, wrote of an occasion shortly after the beginning of the twentieth century, when an elk, having strayed across the border from Russia, was spotted wandering through the imperial hunting domain of Rominten, East Prussia.

The Kaiser ordered out all the automobiles and carriages . . . and that every available person was to serve as beater, His Majesty and the Princess and the ladies being especially invited in that capacity . . .
The car flew along, the Emperor talking volubly about

the Elch and its habits, and his hopes of slaying the confiding creature; and at last we were deposited about eight miles from home on a rather squelchy, marshy piece of ground, where we were met by Baron von Sturnburg and commanded to follow him in perfect silence, the Emperor meanwhile going on in the car in a different direction. After a long damp walk we were all posted at intervals of about a hundred yards along a thick alley of pines, with whispered instructions to stay where we were and prevent the quarry from breaking through, although we all had grave doubts as to our ability to prevent any animal as large as a moose from doing anything it felt inclined. I went up to the gentleman on my left and whisperingly asked what methods I should employ supposing the mighty beast suddenly appeared in front of me, and he indicated a feeble wagging of the hands as being likely to turn it back in the direction of the Emperor's rifle.[1]

Modern science has established that elk are very easy to tame, especially when separated from their mothers at an early age, so it is surprising how seldom we hear of them being ridden or harnessed. There are some exceptions: Olaus Magnus, Archbishop of Uppsala, was the author of a 'History of the Northern People' (*De gentibus septentrionalibus*, Basel, 1567 – though originally published in Rome, 1555, since the archbishop was more or less in exile as a result of the Reformation), which reported that elk were commonly used as draft animals in his native land.

In Sweden, great speed is made by wild asses, or elk, on the snow-covered ice, especially beyond the royal city of

Moose harnessed for work, beside a tepee in Alberta, c. 1916.

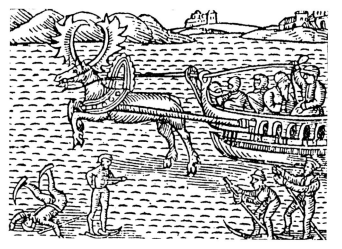

Though moose have seldom been used as beasts of burden, they have often proved surprisingly tractable and easy to break to harness. This illustration of a sledge drawn by a single European elk is from Olaus Magnus's *Historia* . . . (1555) of Northern peoples.

Part of the story of Tycho Brahe and his pet moose, as rendered by the cartoonist Hunt Emerson in his comic strip 'Phenomenomix' for *Fortean Times*, 2007.

Holmen, toward the extreme north. Toward the south, though they are found in large numbers in the great forests, still, on account of a royal edict they are not used, lest traitors employ them, by reason of their speed, which greatly exceeds the speed of horses, to expose the interior of the kingdom to the enemy. This beast endures hunger, thirst and work most patiently, so that in a day and a night he is able to accomplish by running the great distance of 200 Italian miles, without food.[2]

A later historian noted that 'In the reign of Charles IX [of Sweden] elk were made use of for the purpose of conveying couriers, and were capable of accomplishing thirty-six Swedish (about 234 English) [*sic*] miles in a day, when attached to a sledge.'[3] King Charles XI of Sweden himself employed moose-drawn sleighs as his royal courier service. He is also said to have tried to found a moose cavalry, but gave up the experiment when it was discovered that the moose were of too pacific a temperament to be ridden into battle. (Oddly, it is also reported that some horses will panic in the presence of moose; Valerius Geist reports first-hand experience of this strange tendency.)

There are few records of attempts to raise elk as farm animals or objects of biological study; one exception was an anonymous Russian hunter, who acquired two calves in the summer of 1870 and made a close observation of their development. It was also unusual to keep moose as pets, though not unknown. According to his earliest biographer, Pierre Gassendi, no less a figure than the great astronomer Tycho Brahe was an elk-fancier, and engaged in a correspondence on the creature with his aristocratic friend Wilhelm IV, Landgrave of Hesse. In 1591 the Landgrave wrote to Tycho that he had recently been raising a young elk in his deer park at Zapfenburg, and was delighted by its affectionate ways: when Wilhelm went out driving in his green carriage, the young elk would run alongside exactly like a dog. Wilhelm would be delighted, he told his learned friend, if Tycho could supply him with one or two more. Tycho promised to try his best, and explained that he too had kept an elk on his estate in Scania, and had wanted to have it sent over to the base of his astronomical researches in Hveen.

In the first instance, Tycho had the beast transported to Landskrona Castle, where the husband of one of Tycho's nieces was charged with its care. One day, however, the elk found its way into the house, walked up the stairs into a room full of provisions, and drank deeply from a barrel of strong beer. It became so drunk that when it tried to walk back down the staircase it stumbled, broke a leg, and soon perished. Tycho never managed to find any more elk for his friend's deer park.

In 1439, according to his hagiography, the Venerable Macarius of Unzha and his companions were saved from starvation by the appearance of a divinely appointed moose. The holy man's friends were all for falling on the moose and tearing it to shreds, but he restrained them, and told them only to trim a small portion of the moose's ear. This they did; and were all rendered magically immune from hunger for the next three days. After this, the moose returned with others of its kind, and the herd selflessly offered themselves for slaughter and feasting. The miracle is commemorated in a rather fine mosaic.

Perhaps the most curious and widespread of false beliefs about the elk is its association with epilepsy. For centuries, the literate and ignorant alike were convinced that the elk was peculiarly vulnerable to epileptic seizures, and that it could cure itself of the malady by using one of its hind hoofs to open a vein in its ear. By a familiar process of magical thinking, it

The Miracle of the Moose, a mosaic in the Pechersky Ascension Monastery in Nizhny Novgorod, Russia. Note the animal's clipped ear.

Eland

Eland tombé du haut-mal estant pour suivi des Chasseurs.

An elk suffering an epileptic fit, from Pierre Pomet's *Histoire générale des drogues* (1735).

then became believed that humans could be cured of epilepsy by resorting to elk hoof. Olaus Magnus was a firm believer in the efficacy of elks' hooves and gave precise instructions as to procuring the substance. The doctor or patient must, he explains, cut off the outer part of the right hind hoof from the living animal, some time after the middle of August. The great Swiss naturalist Conrad Gesner, writing in 1551, specifies that the elk cures itself by inserting its right hind hoof into its left ear.

This belief endured well into the eighteenth century. One of the most authoritative medical works of its day, the *Histoire générale des drogues* (1735), by Pierre Pomet, repeats Gesner's assertion that the elk's self-surgery requires the insertion of the right hoof into the left ear. Pomet gives a vivid account of how hooves would be gathered. Teams of four men, each armed with an arquebus, would venture into the woods and wait in silence until they saw an elk in the grip of an epileptic seizure. They would fire simultaneously on their quarry, but aim only to wound, not kill. The afflicted elk was then tied town, and the precious rear hoof removed; only then was the creature killed, and cut up for venison.

The heart of the elk-hoof cure was Lithuania, though the trade extended as far south as Italy. Pieces of hoof would be fashioned into rings, and worn on the ring finger of the left

'Female Moose or Elk and Elk's Horns', from Thomas Pennant's *History of Quadrupeds* (1781).

hand; alternatively, fragments of hoof would be set in gold rings or amulets and worn so that the substance was in contact with the finger, chest or neck. Hoofs could also be ingested – they were scraped with a file and sprinkled into wine – or slowly burned so that patients could inhale the fumes.

The epilepsy superstition endured in learned circles until 1784, when Samuel Friedrich Bock explained that observers were misinterpreting the animals' behaviour. The elk was not epileptic, merely itchy; at the season when antlers are shed, the ulcerated area at the base of the horn irritates the poor beast so much that it scratches at the sensitive area so vigorously that it bleeds. Other, later writers have observed that a wounded elk, lying helplessly on the ground waiting for his foe to dispatch him, will strike out again and again with his fore hoofs in a manner that does, indeed, closely resemble an epileptic seizure. Despite the plausibility of these two more rational accounts, the myth continued for many years. Merrill suggests that 'It gained wider currency, and lived more persistently, than any other misbelief associated with any species of animal.'

Other parts of the elk were also harvested for medicinal purposes. If gathered at the appropriate date – around 1 September – the antlers, too, were considered an effective cure for epilepsy. Rings cut from the antlers could be worn to protect against headaches and vertigo, while slices from tender young antlers, mixed together with spirits and herbs, provided a cure for snake bites. The elk's nerves, dried out into long fibres and wrapped around an arm or leg, would provide relief for cramps; elk fat was used as an emollient salve, and so on.

Possibly the oddest folk belief concerns the so-called 'bone' in the elk's heart. In the *Larousse* Dictionary, 'os de coeur de cerf' is cited as an antiquated medical term: 'the bone which is found in the heart of the deer, and which formerly was considered a

'Elke with hornes', from Edward Topsell's *Historie of Foure-footed Beastes* (1607).

powerful therapeutic agent.' Some commentators, not without reason, have assumed that this cardiac 'bone' was entirely fanciful. Yet it does exist: the 'os cordis' is an ossification of the septum between the ventricles of the heart, found in many ruminants (including cows) as they grow old. Though modern science declares its medical value to be nil, European doctors used it for many generations to treat all manner of heart conditions. The superstition appears to have been transported to the New World, mutating en route: Denys records that 'in the heart [of the moose] there is a little bone which the Indian women use to aid them in childbirth, reducing it to powder, and swallowing it in water, or in soup made from the animal.'[4]

Outside the sphere of medicine, a handful of other curious beliefs about the elk prevailed well into the nineteenth century. In his *Allgemeines Tierbuch*, the naturalist Conrad Forer explains that the elk drinks a great deal of water, which he then heats to boiling point in his stomach. When attacked by dogs, wolves or other enemies, he will spew the boiling water over them to drive them away. The English cleric Edward Topsell repeats this notion in his *Historie of Foure-Footed Beastes*:

> When they are chased eagerly and can find no place to rest themselves in and lie secret, they run to the Water and therein stand, taking up water into their mouths, and within short space do heat it, that being squirted or shot out of them upon the Dogs, the heat thereof so oppresseth and scaldeth them, that they dare not once approach or come nigh her any more.[5]

Folk wisdom also had it that, when running through a forest, the elk would tip his head backwards so that his nose would point directly upwards, and his antlers would thus be held clear of low-lying branches. The result: the elk would crash into trees and fall to the ground. Hunters and zoologists doubt the tale.

It was also widely held that elk could successfully and swiftly negotiate swampland by a kind of dog-paddling or swimming motion. In 1817 the German naturalist Georg L. Hartig endorsed this belief – 'Among the peculiarities of this animal it may especially be mentioned that when the ground is very broken and soft he lies down, and seeks to push himself along with his feet.'[6] Later generations of sceptics have pointed out that were this skill so widespread in the species, moose would not so often have been found hopelessly bogged down in marshy ground.

Finally, a curious legend about species enmity. Olaus Magnus reported that the ermine and the moose are sworn foes. 'The ermine often seizes the elk by the throat, and bites them till they bleed to death.' A variant of this yarn is repeated as late as 1838, by Lorenz Oken: 'It is said that the ermine creeps into the elks' ears while they sleep, and bites them so that in their frenzy they dash their heads violently against any object, or throw themselves over a precipice.'[7]

The meaning of the word 'elk' has often been muddied by fancy, false etymology and legend. Here is Topsell:

> This beast is called in Greek Alke, and in Latin Alces, or Alce, which was the name of one of Actaeon's Dogs in Ovid; the Turks, Valachians, the Hungarians, Iaius, the Illirians and Polonians Los, in the singular, and plurally Lossie, for many Elks. Albertus Magnus calleth it Alches and Aloy, and afterwards Equicervus, a Horse-Hart. The Germans, Elch, Ellend, and Elent, by a metathesis of Alke, or Alce; and for my part, I take it to be the same beast which Pliny calleth Machlis [Topsell is correct], for there is nothing attributed to an Elk which also doth not belong to Machlis.[8]

This is not so very far from the account given by the Victorian naturalist Richard Lyddeker, who wrote that 'by the ancient Greeks . . . the great stag we now call the elk was regarded as the personification of strength, and was accordingly named *alce*, from ἄλκη, strength. From this comes the Latin *alces*, the German *Eland*, the French *élan* and the English *elk*.'[9] A nice try; but the true Greek word for 'strength' is ἀλκή, while the word for elk is the similarly spelled, but differently accented ἄλκη. The true root word of *alces* appears to be the Old German *elg* (compare the rune form *algiz*, which looks a little like stylized

The *algiz* rune; in some traditions, it is said to signify an elk.

antlers, and is sometimes said to signify moose or elk), from which actually came the Latin *alces*, the late Greek word ἄλκη, the modern German *Elch* and the English *elk*. In Sweden and Norway the elk continues to be *elg*, in France *élan* – or *orignal* – in Italy *alce* and in Holland *eland*.

Variant German forms of the word once included *Elend* and *Eland*; since *Elend* is also the German word for 'misery', it was long supposed that the name was derived from the elk's melancholic demeanour. Oken, it is charming to note, called the elk 'a melancholy animal', *ein melancholisches Tier*.[10] Thus Topsell:

> The Germans call this Beast Ellend, which in their language signifieth miserable or wretched, and in truth if the report thereof be not false, it is in a most miserable and wretched case, for every day throughout the year it hath the falling sickness.[11]

He goes on to outline the old epilepsy myth. Sadly, the true story is less poetic; other German variants include *Elen*, derived from the Lithuanian *elnis*, meaning a stag; it was this connection rather than melancholia that produced the *Elend*. The German language also contains two more folkloric words for moose: *Moorhirsch* or *Sumpfhirsch*, 'marsh stag'.

Yet this false etymology may have been one reason why Albrecht Dürer, in his magnificent engraving of *Adam and Eve* (*c*. 1504) shows the elk stalking through the trees of Eden. Erwin Panofsky and his disciples in the field of iconography explain that four of the creatures shown in the image represent the four humours: the cat is choleric, the rabbit sanguine, the ox phlegmatic and the elk melancholy. The elk in this work looks so similar to the one depicted by the artist in another portrait

illustrated here that it seems fair to assume that he had only ever enountered the one specimen.

To complicate matters still further, writers quite often used some term signifying, simply, 'big animal' to mean 'moose' or 'elk'. *Animal magnum* is a staple of medieval writers in Latin, and leads to such coinages as *granbestia* in Italian and Spanish and *granbesta* in Portuguese. The thirteenth-century alchemist and mystic Albertus Magnus coined the word *equicervus*, 'horse-deer', for the German *Elch*; and later writers in Latin, misled by the similarity of ear shape in the two distinct species, called the elk an *onager*, or wild ass.

In the twenty-first century, the range of words in different languages denoting 'moose' is impressively varied. Here is a selection – some only roughly transliterated:

Basque	*Altze*
Catalan	*Ant*
Chinese (Mandarin)	*Milu*
Croatian	*Los*
Danish	*Elg*
Dutch	*Eland*
Estonian	*Poder*
Finnish	*Hirvi*
French	*Elan*
French (Canada)	*Orignal*
German	*Elch*
Greek	*Tarandos*
Hebrew	*Ayal Kore*
Hungarian	*Javorszarvas*
Icelandic	*Elgur*
Italian	*Alce*
Japanese	*Musu*
Norwegian	*Elg*
Polish	*Los*
Portuguese	*Alce*
Romanian	*Elan*
Russian	*Los'*
Spanish	*Alce*
Swedish	*Alg*
Yupik	*Tuntua*

The earliest known pictorial representation of the European elk appears to be a prehistoric rock-carving in the valley of the Ussuri, on the Russo-Chinese frontier, not far from the Sea of Japan.[12] Though the legs are a little short and the body markings cryptic, the combination of muzzle shape, antlers and hump are unambiguously alcine. Paintings and carvings of elk forms are particularly abundant in the region that is now called Norway.

While the names of those ancient rock artists are lost forever, the man who left us the first written record of the European elk is one of the great names of world history: Julius Caesar. In his *De bello Gallico* (written in 53 BC, during his second expedition into the land of the Germani), Caesar wrote of a strange animal he had encountered in the great Hercynian forest: 'Sunt item quae appellantur alces . . . Crura sine nodis articulisque habent . . .'. Or, in translation:

> There are also animals which are called *alces* . . . They have legs without joints and ligatures; nor do they lie down for the purpose of rest, nor, if they have been thrown down by any accident, can they raise or lift themselves up. Trees serve them as beds. They lean themselves against them, and thus reclining only slightly they take their rest. When the hunters have discovered from the tracks of these animals whither they are accustomed to go, they either undermine all the trees at the roots, or cut into them so far that the upper part of the trees may appear to be left standing. When they have leaned upon them, according to their habit, they knock down by their weight the unsupported trees, and fall down themselves along with them.[13]

Alerted to the existence of these exotic specimens, the Romans duly set about tracking them down and importing them for use in their favourite pastime: spectacular mass slaughter. In his *Historiae Augustae*, Julius Capitolinus records that among the 5,000-odd exotic beasts set to bloody, fatal combat in the Colosseum in the year AD 244 were 32 elephants,

60 lions, 1 rhinoceros, 30 leopards, 10 giraffes, 20 zebras, 10 tigers . . . and 10 alces.

A century or so after Caesar's pioneering account, Pliny the Elder, in *Naturalis historia*, included alces in his compendium of known species:

> There is, also, the elk, which strongly resembles our steers, except that it is distinguished by the length of ears and of the neck. There is also the achlis, which is produced in the islands of Scandinavia [*nb: translators of Pliny have generally assumed that achlis and elk are one and the same creature*]. It has never been seen in this city, although we have had descriptions of it from many persons; it is not unlike the elk, but it has no joints in the hind leg. Hence, it never lies down, but reclines against a tree while it sleeps; it can only be taken by previously cutting into the tree, and thus laying a trap for it, as otherwise, it would escape through its swiftness. Its upper lip is extremely large, for which reason it is obliged to go backwards while grazing; otherwise, by moving onwards, the lip would get doubled up.'[14]

Pausanias, in his *Description of Greece*, mentions 'the elks, those wild animals in Celtic land'. He notes, more or less correctly, that 'the male elks have horns on their eyebrows, but the females have none at all'.[15] Pliny and Pausanias had few literary heirs until the Renaissance, and the scholarly history of the European elk was not picked up again until the sixteenth and seventeenth centuries, with the likes of Sebastian Münster's *Cosmographia universalis*, first published in Basel in 1544. (About a decade, to put it in context, before the birth of Shakespeare.) Münster describes the elk as being as large as an

ass or a medium-sized horse, with long, weak legs.

In underestimating the average size of an elk, Münster took the opposite tack from most other natural historians, who have been inclined to exaggerate the animal's size. Olaus Worm, also writing in the seventeenth century, said that the animal was so large 'ut sub ventre ejus quis stare valeret' – that one could stand up beneath its belly.[16] Worm also emphasized the extreme timidity of the elk, which took flight at the merest approach of men, and said that the creature's sensibilities were so delicate that it would die in shock at the sight of its own blood, even if the wound were only slight: 'Timidum animal est, adveientes homines fugiens, quovis parvo vulnere moritur, & si suum viderit sanguinem exanimatur.'

The European elk, as depicted in a 1552 edition of Sebastian Münster's *Cosmographia universalis.*

A hundred years later Erich Pontoppidan, Bishop of Bergen, wrote in his *Natural History of Norway* (London, 1755) that elk 'are very long-legged, insomuch that a man may stand upright under their belly'. Pontoppidan was, perhaps, not a great stickler for accuracy or first-hand investigation. His book also describes a local sea serpent that was 600 feet long and capable of raising its head as high as a ship's main-top.

Münster's account maintains that elk are stupid beasts, though tractable enough – a boy can easily drive them along with a stick – but he insists that they cannot be made to carry a rider or other burdens on their back: 'Nec possunt quicquam ferre in dorso'. Their skins, he says, are so tough that they are virtually impossible to cut – a curious belief, but widespread in its day. Their main benefit to humanity is that their hooves

Moose and Reindeer, from the Revd Erich Pontoppidan's *Natural History of Norway* (1755); a useful reminder of the marked differences between the two forms of deer.

A female European elk, after an image in Ulisse Aldrovandi's *Quadrupedum omnium* (1621).

A male European elk, also after Aldrovandi.

provide a medicinal substance that can cure the seriously ill of their maladies.

A later natural historian, Ulisse Aldrovandi – a professor at the University of Bologna – devotes a fair amount of space to *alces*, which he also calls an 'onager' or 'wild ass', in his *Quadrupedum omnium bisulcorum historia* (Bonn, 1621). The illustrations to his work are so approximate as to suggest that the artist was working from hearsay: his portrait of a male elk does indeed look something like an irate ass, with a dreadlock-style dewlap and

Simon Nicholas, *Norwegian Moose*, 1987, oil on canvas.

antlers that, as one sardonic commentator has pointed out, look like minor specimens of the cactus family.

For all practical purposes, the elk was a creature of rumour and myth to most southern and western Europeans for about a thousand years: hence, as noted, those taxonomic errors in the New World. In the twenty-first century Norway, Sweden, Denmark, Finland, the Czech Republic, Estonia, Lithuania, Russia, Siberia, Slovakia and even parts of Poland (where the creature was once hunted almost to extinction) are the home of the European elk; Asian elk survive in Manchuria. From the sixteenth century onwards, though, most of the important developments in moose history took place across the Atlantic, in the New World.

3　The New World Moose

In sixteenth-century Europe, the moose was thought to be one of the more conspicuous marvels of the New World, a creature as rare and improbable as a unicorn. Long before live specimens were shipped back across the Atlantic for the instruction and delight of the learned, explorers sent back racks of antlers as a kind of appetizer. Queen Elizabeth I was the recipient of some five sets of antlers, which she duly displayed in her so-called Horn Room in Hampton Court Palace. They have since been re-located in the Great Room, and may well be the oldest (that is, of a non-fossil kind) collected set of moose antlers anywhere in the world. Samuel Merrill, who visited Hampton Court in the early twentieth century to research for his classic monograph *The Moose Book*, was surprised to note that these moose antlers had been mounted on the carved heads of *Cervus elaphus* (European cousin to the wapiti). Merrill also had some taxidermists measure the antlers, and found that they were of relatively modest proportions compared to living moose, from the largest at 59 inches (150 cm) across down to the tiny 38 in. (97 cm) across. This must have seemed a trifle disappointing to anyone who had read the series of reports on American wildlife, most of which stressed that the moose was a creature of giant dimensions.

As one might expect, reports of moose throughout the early years of colonization are often clouded by terminological

uncertainty. Few of the pioneers were trained scientists; indeed, science as we now understand the term was, at best, in its infancy. And problems of identification are further muddied by the jumble of French, English and other languages in which those reports were written. Sometimes, the only tool for translating words that may signify 'moose' is educated guesswork.

In the few works devoted to this specialized topic, it is usually asserted that the very first European to record his contact with moose is Captain Jacques Cartier. Cartier explored the valley of the St Lawrence as early as 1532, and mentions the wild animals hunted there by the Indians including *dains* and *cerfz*. His translator – Hiram B. Stephens – renders *dains* as 'moose', but admits that he is not sure about the accuracy of the identification. Elsewhere, Cartier mentions buying the meat of 'Cerfs & Dains' from local Indians, and cooking it for his men, who had been unsuccessful in hunting and were dying from scurvy. Cartier reports that the local equivalents of his terms are 'Aiounesta & Asquenodo', though these have never been matched in the word-lists of other travellers.[1]

Many of the early European depictions of moose are clearly based on verbal reports rather than direct observation; this illustration from Theodor de Bry's *Admiranda narratio* (1590) suggests that the artist supposed that a moose resembled a horse with antlers.

Tome 1er Pag. 72

11ᵉ Raquettes

BRAYER

Est un morceau d'Etoffe de
toutes couleurs qu'il passe a une
ceinture de corde, tant par le
devant que par le derriere

Orignaux ou Elans

Other, later reports are equally cloudy. Jean-François de La Roque, Sieur de Roberval, made an attempt to colonize Montreal Island in 1541–2. He mentions some creatures that he calls 'Bugles' – a term that some commentators have identified as 'moose'. Samuel de Champlain (sometimes given the soubriquet 'Father of New France') visited New France in 1603. He borrowed a Basque word, *orignac*, when referring to the moose, apparently – and, for once, correctly – recognizing it as identical with the European elk. A variant form of the word, *orignal*, became common in later accounts, where from time to time it is incorrectly given as 'original' – a chance resemblance that has prompted fanciful etymologies on the theme of alcine originality.

His experiences are recorded in *Les Voyages du Sieur de Champlain* (1613), later translated as *The Savages; or, Voyage of Sieur de Champlain Made in the Year 1603*. He puts the 'orignac' first in a list of twelve animals essential to the subsistence of the Indians. In a later book of 1632, *Les Voyages de la Nouvelle France Occidentale, dicte Canada*, while describing his journeys along the St Croix river, he gives an account of their winter hunting methods. Teams of men, women and children, dressed in beaver and moose skin, would set off on snow-shoes, armed with bows and spears. This is the technique known as 'crusting'.

Champlain also describes an Indian feast, which he witnessed near the mouth of the Saguenay:

> They began their tabagie or feast, which they make with the flesh of the orignac (which is like beef), the bear, seals, and beavers, which are their most common meats, and game birds in quantity. They had eight or ten kettles, full of meat, in the cabin. These were some six paces from each other . . . They eat in a very filthy manner, for when

'Crust hunting', a drawing from Baron Lahontan's *New Voyages to North America* (1703).

their hands are greasy they wipe them on their hair, or on
their dogs, of which they keep many for hunting.

The haziness of these earliest records starts to fade away in
the work of Marc Lescarbot, in whose work the *orignac* is clearly
identified as the moose. Lescarbot of Paris (born *c.* 1570; died
some time after 1629, the date of his last published work) was a
lawyer, poet, Huguenot sympathizer and historian of New France,
to which he travelled from May 1606 and stayed to September
1607, motivated 'by his desire to flee a corrupt world and to
examine this land with his own eyes'. His *Histoire de la Nouvelle-
France* was published in Paris in 1609. At the insistence of Richard
Hakluyt, it was translated – in an edited form – by one Pierre
Erondelle in 1609 as *Nova Francia: A Description of Acadia, 1606.*

First let us speak of the elan, which they [the Indians] call
aptaptou, and our Basques *Orignac* . . .

68

This detail from a map in Gian Battista Ramusio's *Navigationi e viaggi* (1556) is probably the earliest European depiction of a North American moose.

MONTE REAL

It is the tallest creature that is, next unto the dromedary and camel, for it is higher than the horse. His hairs be commonly of grey colour, and sometimes of dun or fallow, almost as long as the fingers of one's hand. His head is very long, and hath almost an infinite order of teeth. He beareth his horns double like the stag, but as broad as a plank, and three feet long, garnished with sprigs growing upward all along upon one side. His feet be forked as the stag's, but much more flat. His flesh is short and very delicate. He feedeth in the meadows, and liveth also of the tender crops of trees. It is the most abundant food which the savages have, next to fish.[2]

Lescarbot spent some time with de Mont's colony in Acadia. On his map of Port Royal, 1609 (now Annapolis Basin, Nova Scotia), he shows the '*R[ivière] de l'Orignac*' – recent maps designate this as Moose River. On the lower margin of the map stands a moose. Merrill thought this the earliest picture of an American moose to come down to us – and it may be that it is the earliest to be based on a personal sighting rather than reports – but there are some possible earlier contenders.

The Italian historian, geographer and statesman Gian Battista Ramusio produced a map and diagram of an Iroquoian village at Hochelaga – the site on which Montreal would grow – published in the third volume of his *Navigationi e viaggi* in 1556. Several animals are depicted to the left side of the plan, including bear, elk and a quadruped with palmate antlers that is almost certainly a moose. However, Ramusio never visited North America; he derived all his knowledge from published accounts, notably Cartier's.

Another second-hand moose portrait was engraved in 1590 by the Flemish goldsmith Theodor de Bry (1528–1598; though the work has sometimes been attributed to the much younger Mattheus Merianus, 1573–1650). The background of his picture shows various hunting methods – some moose are being driven into the water by fires, while others are pursued in canoes by Indians armed with clubs and arrows. The large creature in the foreground looks more like a horse than a moose – it has a short muzzle and a long, luxuriant mane that stretches all along its back – but the antlers are definitely palmate and there appears to be a modest dewlap.

From 1610 onwards, the richest documentary source for the relation of man and moose is the series of reports sent back by Jesuit missionaries – the 'Black Robes'.[3] The *Jesuit Relations*, which in their published and edited version of the late nineteenth century run to no fewer than 73 volumes, are remarkable not only for the range of their reportage and commentary but also for their accuracy. Consisting of the annual reports of missionaries filed from 1610 to 1791, their pages teem with accounts of *l'elan* and *l'orignal*.

As well as their extensive verbal reports on moose, some missionaries also made drawings of the animal. This watercolour sketch, which mistakenly suggests that the moose and the caribou are one and the same beast, is from Louis Nicolas's *Codex Canadensis* (c. 1680–1700).

As Merrill observes:

Like the Indians, the priests were dependent on the
moose for food in winter, and like the Indians they went
hungry when for lack of deep crusted snow the hunters
with their primitive weapons were unable to capture
game. Often they tell of sustaining life by eating acorns,
lichens, and remnants of moose skin, because the hunt
had failed.

In other words, the moose thus played an important, even a crucial role in the transmission of Christianity in Canada. We have
vivid accounts of just how harsh life could be for the Black Robes
when the moose hunt failed. Here is Father Bressani, in 1653:

The snow not being deep, as in other years, they could
not take the great beasts [*gran bestie* = moose] but only
some beavers or porcupines . . . An eelskin was deemed a
sumptuous supper; I had used one for mending my robe,
but hunger obliged me to unstitch and eat it. We ate the
dressed skins of the great beast, though tougher than
that of the eels. I would go into the woods to gnaw the
tenderest parts of the trees, and the softer bark . . . The
snow came towards the end of January, and our hunters
captured some great beasts, and smoked their flesh, so
much that it became as hard as a stick of wood . . .
Meanwhile some of the Indians in the neighbourhood
died of starvation.[4]

The Jesuits also recorded a widespread belief – one that will
by now be familiar – that elk and moose were subject to epilepsy, but could cure themselves by scratching their ear with the

left hind hoof until the ear bled. Hence, human sufferers from epilepsy were told to take the chopped-off hoof of a moose in their left hand and rub their ear with it. In other words, Native American folklore seemed identical on this point to European folklore. Father Joseph Jouvency attests to the belief:

> In this hoof there is a certain marvellous and manifold virtue, as is affirmed by the testimony of the most famous physicians. It avails especially against the epilepsy, whether it be applied to the breast, where the heart is throbbing, or whether it be placed in the bezel of a ring, which is worn upon the finger next to the little finger of the left hand; or, finally, if it be also held in the hollow of the left hand, clenched in the fist. Nor does it have less power in the cure of pleurisy, dizziness, and, if we may believe those familiar with it, six hundred other diseases.[5]

The fanciful conclusion is that the moose hoof really does have curative powers; the more likely explanation is that the Native Americans had somehow picked up this belief from the colonists, and that the Jesuits were unwittingly reporting on a European import as though it were an exotic peculiarity.

In 1625 Samuel Purchas published his great folios of recent travel narratives with the collective title *Purchas His Pilgrimes*; and some of these narratives include sightings of moose. The earliest published mention of a moose in any English text appears to be in an edition of *Purchas His Pilgrimes*: 'Captaine Thomas Hanham sayled to the Riuer of Sagadahoc, 1606. He relateth of their beasts . . . redde Deare, and [a] beast bigger, called the Mus.' Purchas also quotes from Sir Ferdinando Gorges, *A Brief Relation of the Discovery and Plantation of New England* (1622):

There is also a certaine Beast, that the Natives call a *Mosse*, hee is as big bodied as an Oxe . . . His taile is longer than the Single of a Deere, and reacheth almost downe to his Huxens [Hocks] . . . There have beene many of them seene in a great Iland upon the Coast, called by our people *Mount Mansell* [today Mount Desert Island, Maine], whither the Savages goe at certaine seasons to hunt them [by driving them into the water] . . . And there is hope that this kind of Beasts may be made serviceable for ordinary labour, with Art and Industry.

The next few years saw the publication of many similar reports. In 1630 the Revd Francis Higginson wrote of 'a great beast called a Molke as bigge as an Oxe'. In 1634 William Wood (fl. 1629–35) published *New England's Prospect*, a study of the region and its wildlife in both prose and poetry, based on four years of residence:

The kingly Lyon, and the strong arm'd Beare
The large lim'd Mooses, with the tripping Deare,
Quill darting Porcupines, and Rackoones bee,
Castelld in the hollow of an aged tree . . .[6]

Expanding, species by species, on each of the beasts he mentions, Wood goes on to explain that

The beast called a Moose is not much unlike red deer. This beast is as big as an ox, slow of foot, headed like a buck, with a broad beam, some being two yards wide in the head. Their flesh is as good as beef, their hides good for clothing. The English have some thoughts of keeping them tame and to accustom them to the yoke, which will be a great commodity; first because they are so fruitful, bring-ing forth three at a time [*sic*], being likewise very uberous [supplying milk or nourishment in abundance]; secondly, because they will live in winter without fodder. There be not many of these in the Massachusetts Bay, but forty miles to the northeast there be great store of them. These poor beasts likewise are much devoured by the wolves.[7]

Thomas Morton, a sometime lawyer of Clifford's Inn, London, notorious roisterer and keen hunter, wrote of 'tenne yeares knowledge and experiment of the Country' in his *New English Canaan* of 1637. He was a keen enough observer to discriminate between the three kinds of deer he had met:

First therefore I will speak of the Elke, which the Salvages [savages] call a Mose: it is a very large Deare, with a very faire head, and a broade palme, like the palme of a fallow Deares horne, but much bigger, and is 6. foot wide betweene the tipps, which grow curbing downwards: Hee is of the bignesse of a great horse.

There have bin of them, seene that has bin 18. hand-fulls high: hee hath a bunch of hair under his jawes; he is not swifte, but stronge and large in body, and longe legged; in somuch that he doth use to kneele, when hee feedeth on grasse.

Hee bringeth forth three faunes, or younge ones, at a time; and being made tame, would be good for draught, and more usefull (by reason of their strength) than the Elke of Raushea.[8]

Morton was far from alone in speculating about the possibility of domesticating and training moose, and the experiment was occasionally tried. Father Le Jeune, superior of the Residence of Kebec, wrote in 1636 that the French Governor was holding two bulls and a cow moose in captivity and attempting to train them. There is no word as to the outcome, but – as episodes from Swedish and Russian history have proved – it is not too hard to break moose to the halter, if much more difficult to train them to be ridden like horses.

Though a relatively neglected figure in histories of New World naturalists, Pierre Boucher was among the earliest visitors to attempt an exhaustive description of all the flora and fauna in a given region, and his *Histoire veritable et naturelle* of 1664 was an admirable work that anticipated the better-known surveys undertaken decades later by the likes of the Bartrams, Catesby, the Audubons, Wilson and Lawson.

> Let us begin with the most common and most natural of all animals in this country, the 'Elan', which is called in these parts 'Original' [*sic*]. They are normally bigger than large mules with a head shaped more or less the same. The difference is that the males have antlers similar to the deer, but flat. These fall off every year and each year add one new fork. The flesh is good and light and never does any harm. The skin is worn in France and passes for buffalo, the bone marrow has medicinal value for nerve ailments. It is said that the hoof of the left foot is good for the illness 'caduc'. [That is, epilepsy.] It is an animal with long legs and a good disposition. It has a split hoof, and no tail. It defends itself with its front hoofs like a deer.

'HERE BEFORE CHRIST': THE HUDSON'S BAY COMPANY

Far and away the most important of the early commercial enterprises to operate within moose ranges was the legendary Hudson's Bay Company. It was chartered on 2 May 1670 by King Charles II, and, despite the harshness of the terrain in which it was operating and the competition from other trading companies, it enjoyed a triumphant rise. Though, in its first years, the company was not primarily concerned with hunting moose as a commercial product – beaver fur was a far more profitable commodity – its reliance on moose meat for food and moose hide for clothing was such that figures of rampant moose were displayed on its coat of arms.

As Franzmann puts it, 'figuratively speaking, the moose was the fuel for all the Company's far-flung endeavours'.[9] Moose flesh fed both company employees and the natives who came to trade at its factories and outposts. In the larger HBC posts, local hunters would be employed to keep up a steady supply of moose flesh. (The rival Northwest Fur Company, which traded to the south in the Great Lakes area and the St Lawrence River, was similarly dependent on moose meat.)

Moose skins were used to make 'toggies' or 'banians', long, loose-fitting outer garments that hung down to just above the ankles, worn by HBC men in wintertime. Plucked moose skins were also used to cover the windows of the company's forts and other outposts, since they reduced the wind but allowed the passage of at least a little light.

Then, gradually, changes in the demand for particular types of skin modified the company's policy on moose hunting. On 30 May 1694 the HBC governor James Knight was told:

Moose skins or *Buffelo hydes* are a great commodity here this Warr time,[10] therefore if any are to be had pray send them home & suffer them not to be used in the Factory Upon any accott. whatsoever haveing sent Leather &ca.

to Supply in stead thereof . . . Wee must alsoe Perticulerly recommend to you the Improvement of . . . procuring all the Moose Skins you can & not suffer any of them to be cutt or otherwise used in the Factory . . .[11]

Various attempts were made to establish a rate of exchange between moose hides and other commodities, with the 'made beaver' – a whole skin taken from an adult beaver in first-rate condition – as the universal trading unit. It may be that the name of the well-known HBC trading post on James Bay, Moose Factory, reflects the importance of the species to Company fortunes, but it is more likely that it took its name from the place on which it was sited: the mouth of Moose River, Ontario. This was the ancient home of the Monsoni, or 'Moose People', an Algonquin tribe closely related to the Crees and the Chippewas, who adopted the moose as their totem.

THE NEXT WAVE OF NATURAL HISTORIANS

The Dutch savant Arnoldus Montanus addressed the moose question in his study of 1671, *The New and Unknown World; or, Description of America and the Southern Land* (*De Nieuwe en Onbekende Weereld: of Beschryving van America en 't Zuid-Land*). His is a slightly fanciful account, which repeats quite a few elements of the now-familiar folklore:

South [*sic*] of New Netherland are found numerous elks (*eelanden*), animals which, according to Erasmus Stella [author of an early sixteenth-century tract on the Prussian elk], constitute a middle class between horses and deer. They appear to derive their Dutch appelation from *elende* [misery], because they die of the smallest

wound, however strong they may otherwise be; also, because they are frequently afflicted with epilepsy . . . When hunted they spew hot water out on the dogs. They possess great strength of hoof, so as to strike a wolf dead at a blow. Their flesh, either fresh or salted, is very nutritious; the hoofs cure the falling sickness.

It should not come as much of a surprise to learn that Montanus also maintained that the unicorn was a native of the Canadian borderlands.

Vignette of a moose, from John Ogilby's *America: Being the Latest, and Most Accurate Description of the New World* (1671), an English version of Arnoldus Montanus's *De Nieuwe en Onbekende Weereld* of the same year.

A considerably more sober and reliable source of enlightenment came in the form of two important works by John Josselyn. *New Englands Rarities Discovered* of 1672, and *An Account of Two Voyages to New England* of 1674.

From the former:

> Their flesh is not dry like Deers flesh, but moist and lushious somewhat like Horse flesh (as they judge that have tasted of both) but very wholsome. The flesh of their *Fawns* is an incomparable dish, beyond the flesh of an Asses foal so highly esteemed by the *Romans*, or that of young Spaniel Puppies so much cried up in our days in *France* and *England*.

From the latter:

> The *Moose* or *Elke* is a Creature, or rather if you will a Monster of superfluity. A full grown *Moose* is many times bigger than an *English* Oxe, their horns as I have said elsewhere, very big (and branct out into palms) the tips whereof are sometimes found to be two fathom asunder (a fathom is six feet from the tip of one finger to the tip of the other, that is four cubits), and in height from the toe of the forefoot, to the pitch of the shoulder twelve foot, both which have been taken by some of my *sceptique* Readers to be monstrous lies.

Josselyn's accounts of the Moose were taken so seriously that they were published in the *Philosophical Transactions* of the Royal Society. But they did not pass uncriticized. In 1721 Paul Dudley published his paper *A Description of the Moose-Deer in America*, which takes issue with Josselyn's accuracy. Dudley was a man of considerable standing: a Fellow of the Royal Society and Chief Justice of the Province of Massachusetts Bay, he was a leading citizen of Roxbury, which today is part of Boston. Calling Josselyn's account 'imperfect', he begins by drawing distinctions:

> Of Moose there are two sorts, the Common light grey moose, by the Indians called Wampoose [that is, the wapiti]; these are more like the ordinary Deer, spring like them, and herd sometimes to thirty in a Company. And then there are the large, or black Moose, of which I shall now give you the following account. First, That he is the Head of the Deer-kind, has many things in Common with other deer, in many things differs, but in all very superiour . . . He has a very short Bob for a Tail. Mr Neal, in his late History of this Country, speaking of the Moose, says they have a long Tail; but that Gentleman was imposed upon, as to other things beside the Moose . . . [12]

Nicholas Denys was among the first amateur naturalists to record a drastic decline in moose numbers. He had worked successfully in the fishing and timber trading business, and eventually became a governor of part of Acadia. His classic work of 1672, *Description geographique et historique des costes de L'Amerique septentrionale*, was translated into English in 1908 as *The Description and Natural History of the Coasts of North America*. Denys came into close contact with the Micmac tribe, and his book offers one of the fullest and most minutely observed accounts of the Native American techniques of moose hunting. (He stresses that his accounts refer to the years 1600–1640 – well before 'le debasement culturel' of these peoples.) He then noted of Cape Breton Island that

This island has also been esteemed for the hunting of moose. They were found formerly in great numbers but at present there are no more. The Indians have destroyed everything, and have abandoned the island, finding there is no longer the wherewithal for living.[13]

At first sight, this should make uncomfortable reading for those who subscribe to the belief that the Native American people had developed a complex and spiritually rich rapport with the animals they hunted, which ensured ecological harmony. But if that view is a trifle too roseate, it still seems plain enough that the new levels of slaughter were carried out precisely to meet cravings that had been introduced by the Europeans. Indians were generally paid for moose skins in French brandy. The death rate escalated rapidly, since these skins were greatly in demand for the production of the soft but hard-wearing uncoloured buff leather. Commenting on the territory at the head of the Bay of Fundy, Denys also notes that 'The Sieur d'Aunay in his time [1645–50] traded in moose skins there to the extent of 3000 skins a year . . . which was the reason why he dispossessed the Sieur de la Tour of it.'

By the end of the 1660s moose were being slaughtered in such numbers that the price of their flesh plummeted. The *Journals of Dollier and Galinee, 1669–70* records that 'Meat is so cheap here [probably in the region of Sault Ste Marie] that for a pound of glass beads I had four minots of fat entrails of moose, which is the best morsel of the animal. This shows how many these people kill.'[14]

Jesuits continued to observe that moose were being hunted to extinction in some areas: Father Sebastien Rasle, writing to his brother from Narantsouak (now Norridgewock, Maine) on 12 October 1723, said that 'Our savages have so destroyed the game of their country that for ten years they have no longer either moose [*orignaux*] or deer [*chevreuil*]. Bears and beavers have become very scarce. They seldom have any food but Indian corn, beans, and squashes.' (Father Rasle himself died less than a year later.)[15]

By the early eighteenth century some regions were so depleted of their former moose stocks that it would not have seemed fanciful to predict the extinction of the beast within much of its former North American range. In 1721 Pierre de Charlevoix bemoaned the uncontrolled slaughter of recent years:

> let us now return to our hunting; that of the moose would be no less advantageous to us than that of the beaver, had our predecessors in the colony paid due attention to the profits which might have been made by it, and had they not almost entirely destroyed the whole species, at least in such places as are within our reach.[16]

From William Daniell's *Interesting Selections from Animated Nature* (1809); depictions of moose remained mildly fanciful well into the 19th century.

Warnings of this nature came too late for many districts. And in the more remote areas, where moose continued to abound despite the best efforts of hunters, the slaughter would continue for the better part of two hundred years. Yet all the evidence suggests that the balance of human and moose populations had been fairly stable for countless years, probably centuries, before the colonists arrived.

THE MOOSE AND NATIVE AMERICANS

What the Buffalo was to the Plains, the Whitetail Deer to the Southern woods, and the Caribou to the Barrens, the Moose is to this great Northern belt of swamp and timberland . . . It is the creature that enables the natives to live.[17]

It is hard to overstate the role that moose played in the lives of the more northerly indigenous peoples. In the most hazardous months of the year, moose flesh was not simply a staple diet, but (with the sole exception of caribou meat) also the only significant source of nourishment. Franzmann puts it bluntly: 'In much of northern forested America, human existence essentially depended on the moose.'[18] Because of their healthy fertility rates and wide dispersion through the forest lands, moose easily withstood the relatively modest depletion of the numbers by native hunting methods. Had moose not thrived, the tribes would have been forced to migrate to the south or simply perish.

According to the Smithsonian's *Handbook of American Indians*, published in 1910, the principal variations in names of the moose were:

Narraganset and Massachset   *moos*
Delaware   *mos*

Passamaquoddy	*mus*
Abnaki	*monz*
Chippewa	*mons*
Cree	*monswa*
Montagnais	*moosh*

'All of these words signify "he strips or eats off," in reference to the animal's habit of eating the young bark and twigs of trees.'

Since few Native Americans of this period learned to read and write, we owe most of our knowledge of their interactions with moose to the reports of settlers and travellers. One of the best descriptions of native hunting methods, for example, was composed by John Giles (1677–1755) of Pemaquid, Maine. Giles was taken into captivity by a local tribe at the age of twelve, and held for six years, when he was sold by the Indian master to a minor French official, who released him two years later. His command of local languages opened up a career as an army interpreter, and he eventually reached the rank of captain. Giles was also the builder and commander of Fort George, Brunswick; his *Memoirs of Odd Adventures, Strange Deliverances, etc.* was published almost a century after his death, in 1869.

When the winter came on we went up the river until the ice came down, running thick in the river, when, accord-ing to the Indian custom, we laid up our canoes until spring. Then we travelled, sometimes on the ice, and sometimes on the land, till we came to a river that was open, but not fordable, where we made a raft and passed over, bag and baggage. I met with no abuse from them in this winter's hunting, though I was put to great hardships in carrying burdens and for want of food, But they under-

A Cree hunter calling a moose in the American woods, c. 1927.

went the same difficulty, and would often encourage me, saying in broken English, 'By and by great deal moose . . .'

If any disaster had happened, we must all have perished. Sometimes we had no manner of sustenance for three or four days; but God wonderfully provides for all creatures. In one of these fasts, God's providence was remarkable. Our two Indian men who had guns, in hunting, started a moose, but there being a shallow crusted snow on the ground, and the moose discovering them, ran with great force into a swamp. The Indians went round the swamp, and finding no track, returned at night to the wigwam and told what had happened. The next morning they followed him on the track, and soon found him, lying on the snow. He had, in crossing the roots of a large tree that had been blown down, broken through the ice made over the water in the hole occasioned by the roots of the tree taking up the ground, and hitched one of his hind legs among the roots so fast that by striving to get it out, he pulled his thigh bone out of its socket by the hip, and thus extraordinarily were we provided for in our great strait.

Bernard R. Ross of the HBC outlined some of the uses that locals made of the non-edible parts of a moose corpse in his report of 1861, 'An account of the animals useful in an economic point of view to the various Chipewyan tribes':

The hide supplies parchment, leather, lines, and cords; the sinews yield thread and glue; the horns serve for handles to knives and awls, as well as to make spoons of; the shank bones are employed as tools to dress leather with; and with a particular portion of the hair, when died, the Indian women embroider garments . . .

The capotes, gowns, firebags, mittens, moccasins, and trousers made of it are often richly ornamented with quills and beads, and when new look very neat and becoming . . .

One of the few common products that Ross does not mention in his report is the manufacture of small river boats from moose rawhide.

MYTHOLOGY

It is a striking fact that, given the immense significance of moose in the daily life of Native American peoples, there is very little in the way of potent mythology or memorable art devoted to the creature and its ways. Many encylopaedias and dictionaries of Native American culture do not even contain an entry for the word 'moose' – and this despite the fact that some tribes, as we have seen, adopted the moose as their totem animal.

Of the few stories that are worth the telling, the principal ones refer to the origins of the species. More than one tribe, observing how moose would take to the water when threatened, and could sometimes be seen swimming quite far out to sea, quite reasonably postulated that it was originally an aquatic or even an entirely marine creature. In *The Maine Woods*, Thoreau tells of his conversation with the 89-year-old Penobscot, Governor Neptune, who told him that

> He could remember when the moose were much larger; that they did not use to be in the woods, but came out of the water, as all deer did. Moose was whale once. Away down Merrimack way a whale came ashore in a shallow bay. Sea went out and left him, and he came up on land a moose. What made them know he was whale was that, at first, before he began to run in bushes, he had no bowels inside, but – and then the squaw who sat on the bed by his side, as the Governor's aid, and had been putting in a word now and then confirming the story, asked me what we called that soft thing we find along the seashore. 'Jelly-fish,' I suggested. 'Yes,' said he, 'no bowels, but jelly-fish'.[19]

In his *Sporting Adventures in the New World* (London, 1855), Campbell Hardy says that the Micmacs of Nova Scotia were also of the belief that moose originated in the ocean, and that when they are hunted too vigorously they take to the waves again.

Other myths tried to account for the beast's more prominent

physical idiosyncrasies. The Abenakis held that *Glooskap* – their creator god and giant guardian of the Indian race – made the moose huge, but, seeing that the beast was thus too large and too strong to be hunted, took the creature up in his giant hand and squeezed it down to a smaller scale – but squeezed it unevenly, so that it ended up with a humped back, short body and vast nose. The Micmac shared this belief; hence some elegaic – if not very distinguished – verses by the white man Arthur Wentworth Eaton:

> Glooskap it was who taught the use
> Of the bow and the spear, and sent the moose
> Into the Indian hunter's hands;
> Glooskap who strewed the shining sands
>
> Of the tide-swept beach of the stormy bay
> With amethysts purple and agates gray,

George Heriot's *Moose Deer of North America*, an early 19th-century engraving.

And brought to each newly-wedded pair
The Great Spirit's benediction fair.

But the white man came, and with ruthless hand
Cleared the forests and sowed the land,
And drove from their haunts by the sunny shore
Micmac and moose, forevermore.

In a closely related myth, the earliest moose were so large
that they could graze on the tops of trees, and their movements
were a hazard to all smaller species. So the Great Spirit sent a
messenger – *Ksiwhambeh* – to tell the people that he was going
to put an end to this threat. *Ksiwhambeh* took a strip of birch
bark and made a horn from it, with which he summoned the
moose. When the moose arrived, *Ksiwhambeh* informed it that
he was going to make it smaller; the moose placidly lowered its
head, *Ksiwhambeh* took hold of it between the antlers and
crushed it down to its present size. He then sent it off into the
woods, telling it never to come close to man again unless
called.[20]

But by the end of the seventeenth century the age of mythology was about to be put aside by most of the keener minds of
the day, and the study of myth would not flourish again until
the rise of anthropology and related disciplines some two centuries later. In the meantime, the moose would increasingly
become an object of natural philosophical study, as well as the
target of the huntsman's rifle.

4 The Enlightenment Moose

Samuel Johnson's *Dictionary* (1755) is curt on the subject of moose: 'the large American deer; it is the largest of the species of deer.' On the elk, he is more forthcoming:

a large stately animal of the stag kind. The neck is short and slender; the ears nine inches in length, and four in breadth. The colour of its coat in Winter is greyish, in Summer it is paler; generally three inches in length, and equalling horse hair in thickness. The upper lip of the elk is large. The articulations of its legs are close, and the ligaments hard, so that its joints are less pliable than those of other animals. The horns of the male elk are short and thick near the head, where it by degrees expands into a great breadth, with prominences in its edges. Elks live in herds, and are very timorous. The hoof of the left hinder foot only, has been famous for the cure of epilepsies; but it is probable that the hoof of any other animal will do as well.

This is admirable: concise, largely accurate – moose tend to be solitary, not herd creatures – judicious and sceptical, with just the right tang of dead-pan wit. (For 'do as well', we should read 'be every bit as useless.') We are witnessing the consolidation of a new sensibility here, sober, rational, empirical. An intriguing possibility: might Johnson, who died in 1784, have ever seen a North American moose at first hand? Boswell is silent on the point, but it is quite possible that Johnson might have witnessed, and all but certain that he had heard news of, the Canadian moose that was sent to King George III in 1767, which was given a new home in Richmond Park. (Another leading man of letters, Horace Walpole, also saw a moose, at the estate of his nephew, Lord Orford, in 1773.) The moose was no longer a traveller's tale, a legend, a curiosity; now it was the object of scientific study. The crucial figure in this transition is Pehr Kalm.

Kalm (1716–1779) was the first European visitor to North America to be highly trained in the modern school of rigorous observation – we might say, the first visitor who was a scientist. The young Swedish scholar travelled in America from 1747 to 1751. A pupil and later colleague of Carl von Linné, aka Linnaeus, Kalm was – like other savants – keenly interested in the question of whether there might be some connection between the moose and the fossil remains of large antlers found in Ireland.

On 11 November 1747, writing in Philadelphia, Kalm reflects that:

In several writings [Kalm was familiar with Paul Dudley's paper on the American 'Moose-Deer' published in 1721] we read of a large animal, which is to be found in New England and other parts of North America. They sometimes dig very long and branched horns out of the ground in Ireland, and nobody in that country or anywhere else in the world knows an animal which has such horns. This has induced many people to believe that it is the moose-deer so famous in North America, and that the horns found were of animals of this kind which had formerly lived in that island but gradually become extinct. It has even been concluded that Ireland in distant ages was either connected to North America or that a number of little islands which are lost at present made a chain between them. This led me to enquire whether an animal with such excessive great horns as are ascribed to the moose-deer had ever been seen in any part of this country. Mr Bartram [an autodidact who specialized in botany and other branches of natural philosophy] told me that notwithstanding he had carefully enquired to that purpose, yet there was no person who could give him any information which could be relied upon, and therefore he was entirely of the opinion that there was no such animal in North America.

Next, Kalm turned to no less an authority than Benjamin Franklin, the intellectual leader of the colonists. Franklin told him

that he had, when a boy, seen two of the animals which they call Moose-deer, but he well remembered that they were not of such size as they must have been, if the horns found in Ireland were to fit them. The two animals which he saw, were brought to Boston to be sent to England to Queen Anne. Anyone who wanted to see them had to pay twopence. A merchant paid for a number of school-boys who wanted to see them, among whom was Franklin. The height of the animal up to its back was that of a pretty tall horse, but its head and its horns were still higher.

Kalm remained sceptical on the Irish elk question, but correctly guessed that the 'Originals' (*sic*) spoken of by the French Canadians were the same moose-deer of which Dudley had written.

Thomas Jefferson (1743–1826), best remembered as a Founding Father of the United States of America and as its third president, was also one of his age's outstanding scholars and, like many brilliant men of his period, a polymath. 'Natural history is my passion', he once confessed, and it is in his role as a natural historian that he enters the story of the moose. (Theodore Roosevelt was to be the next president with strong alcine interests; but for the greater part of his life, the founder of the Bull Moose Party preferred slaying moose to studying them.) Jefferson had been annoyed by the words of George-Louis Leclerc, Comte de Buffon, at that time widely acknowledged as the world's leading zoologist.

Until the mid-1780s, Buffon had not been able to study a whole specimen of *Alces alces* at first hand, though his American contacts had sent him moose antlers, skeletons and skins. He finally had the chance to examine a European elk at close range in March 1784, when a specimen – a three-year-old, said to have been captured 'fifty leagues beyond Moscow' – was exhibited at the fair of St Germain, near Paris. Buffon had a steel engraving of the creature made up for his *Histoire naturelle*, but improved slightly on nature by adding antlers to the head. The engraving was made in March, and these (or so the showman told Buffon) were the antlers that the creature had shed the previous January.[1]

For a variety of reasons, Buffon contended that when an

A female elk from Buffon's *Histoire naturelle.*

94

Pl. VIII.

Buvée del.

C.E.Fritzsch. fc.

L'ÉLAN.

animal species was found in both the Old and the New World, the New World form was inevitably smaller and usually inferior in other ways. Thomas Jefferson, his patriotism stung, jumped to the defence, and chose the moose as his test case. He turned to the pages of Kalm, and noted that

> Kalm tells us that the Moose . . . of America is as high as a tall horse; and Catesby, that it is about the bigness of a middle sized ox. (I have seen a skeleton 7 feet high, and from good information believe that they are often considerably higher. The elk of Europe is not two-thirds of his height).[2]

Jefferson pursued his research by sending out a sixteen-point questionnaire to everyone he knew who had some competence in the subject. Here are a few of them, with a sampling of answers as supplied by a Mr John McDuffee of Rochester, New York, dated 5 March 1784:

1. [Q.] Is not the Caribou and the Black Moose one and the same animal?
   [A.] The Carabou Calevan or Indian Shovler is an Animal very different from the Moose. His hoofs are like a Horses his Horns are short and have no prongs, is about the bigness of a small Horse, lives in Heaths and Swamps, feeds chiefly on Roots which he digs up with his feet, is seldom seen in this quarter of the country.

2. [Q.] Is not the grey Moose and the Elk one and the same Animal and quite different from the former?
   [A.] The Elk is Deer of a large size and is known by the

name of the Newfoundland Deer. The Black and Grey
Moose are one and the same Animal. The Black are
mostly to be found to the Eastward, the Grey to the
Southward.

3. [Q.] What is the height of the grey Moose at the
    weathers, its length from the Ears in the root of the
    Tail, and its circumference where largest?
    [A.] One of the largest is about 8½ feet high at the
    weathers, 8½ or 9 feet long, behind his fore legs is
    about 7 feet in circumference . . .

And so on. McDuffee completes his questionnaire with a
charming detail: 'Sir, The above answers are the best I am able
to give to your Queries, would only observe that there is a
Moose's Horn in one of the Pigwackett Towns so large that it
is used as a cradle to rock the Children in. Am Sir with due
respects your most Humble Servant, John McDuffee.'

Not all the answers were wholly accurate, but when put
together and edited they provided Jefferson with overwhelming

The skeleton of a
moose, displayed by
Thomas Jefferson to
a group of sceptical
French savants,
including Buffon,
as proof of the
immense size
reached by North
American mammals;
from the 1995
Merchant-Ivory film
Jefferson in Paris.
The skeleton tracked
down by the film's
resourceful art
department proved
to be the very same
one that Buffon
had been sent.

A stuffed moose in a well-known Paris taxidermy shop, 2004.

proof that Buffon's contention was wrong. He also sent Buffon the skin and skeleton of a once-healthy moose to support his case (though these arrived in poor condition after a four-month journey to Paris). Buffon was gracious in defeat: 'I should have consulted you, sir, before publishing my natural history, and then I should have been sure of my facts.'

The entrance hall to Jefferson's self-designed house Monticello, south of Charlottesville, was a small museum of natural history that included a mastodon jaw, a bison skull and moose antlers. It has been suggested that these antlers may have been sent back from the Lewis and Clark expedition.[3] It is a moot point. There is no mention anywhere in Meriwether Lewis's journals of a moose being taken, though several were encountered and one wounded by Reubin Field on 7 July 1805, near the site of Lincoln, Montana. But Lewis's journals cover only 442 of the expedition's 863 days, so it is entirely possible that one or more moose may have been killed en route.

STUBBS'S MOOSE

The single most famous, and by many reckonings the finest, depiction of a North American moose in all European art is *The Duke of Richmond's First Bull Moose*, painted in 1770 by George Stubbs (1724–1806), best known for his enduringly popular studies of horses. The bull moose in question had been sent as a present from the Governor-General of Canada to the Duke of Richmond, who had expressed an interest in the possibilities of breeding the creature in England. The young moose owes his immortality to the great Irish Elk Debate.

William Hunter (1718–1783) suspected that this quadruped might further his researches into the question of whether certain animal species had become extinct, a suggestion that was offensive to many of his contemporaries, since it denied divine providence. His notes report that the moose, a yearling, was 'the first male I believe that ever was seen in Great Britain' – for a number of female moose had already arrived, and other bull moose were to follow in 1772 and 1773.

Hunter obtained 'leave [from the duke] to have a Picture of it

George Stubbs,
*The Duke of
Richmond's First
Bull Moose*, 1770,
oil on canvas. A
rare instance of a
moose portrait by
a major artist.

made by Mr Stubbs, in the execution of which, no pains were spared by that great Artist to exhibit an exact resemblance both of the young animal itself, and of a pair of Horns of the full-grown Animal, which the General had likewise brought from America and presented to the Duke.' Stubbs acted swiftly, for his painting was completed within four months of the yearling's arrival in September 1770.

What Hunter was keen to find out was whether or not the Canadian animal would eventually develop antlers comparable in size to those of the 'elk' fossils found in Ireland. He was fairly sure that the Irish elk was extinct – he had already proved to his own satisfaction that the mastodon was extinct – but needed to establish whether or not 'The Orignal from Quebec', as he called it in his notes, was in fact a living example of the same species. He intended to publish his report in the *Philosophical Transactions of the Royal Society*, but – with admirable scruple – in the end decided not to publish, since all the bull moose he could study first-hand were too young to indicate what a fully mature male might grow on his brow. But his researches were not wholly in vain: he seems to have been full of admiration for Stubbs's meticulous accuracy, and his notes on the youthful moose are a charming compound of precise observation and affectionate interest:

Food. He was very fond of Apples, of bread, of Bran, of some herbs, particularly clover, both fresh and dry, and of the leaves of most trees and shrubs. He would eat, but did not much relish Otes; and he would not taste grass not Hay, nor straw. He drank slowly. He ruminates . . .

Motion. His walk was grave & slow; his Trot swift or rapid, and attended with a smart cracking noise, either from his hoofs or joints . . .

Manners. He appeared to be more intelligent, more grave, & docile than a Horse of the same Age, and less apt to be offended. He knew his keeper, and there was a very sincere and mutual friendship between them: but he was so little shy of strangers, that he would follow anybody who would shew him a piece of bread or an Apple . . .

When he is a little teized with stroaking or rubbing, or only touched by a stranger, he makes a whining or moaning noise through his Throat & Nose, exactly like the sound of a sick or peevish child . . .

The Heat of the weather was supposed to oppress

him; & therefore his keeper had been instructed to throw a Pale-full of water over him now & then to cool him. He appeared to be pleased with it, and always shook himself after it exactly as a horse does when wet or dirty . . . [4]

The Duke of Richmond took delivery of a second bull moose in October 1773. There is a drawing of this creature that was included by Hunter as part of his bequest to the University of Glasgow in 1783; it is generally attributed to Stubbs. An engraving by Peter Mazell of this sketch, used in Thomas Pennant's *Arctic Zoology*, vol. I (1785), bears the inscription 'G Stubbs Del', but some art historians have questioned the attribution, on the grounds that its quality is too poor. (The eminent naturalist Sir Joseph Banks examined the same animal, and had it sketched by John Frederick Miller.) Hunter carefully recorded

George Stubbs, *The Duke of Richmond's Second Bull Moose*, 1773, pencil drawing.

A bull moose – obviously after Stubbs's *Duke of Richmond's First Bull Moose*, though not attributed; from Thomas Pennant's *Arctic Zoology* (1792).

the principal differences between this mature male and the yearling: chief among them were the pendulous 'bell' or 'caruncle' hanging from the throat, 'whose extremity when the hair was burned off was round'; maturing antlers 'dividing into an ascending and descending broad branch'; and 'remarkably long and awkward hoofs on the forefeet'.

Stubbs's depiction of a moose has seldom, if ever, been rivalled for artistry, though over the course of the next eighty years or so at least two other images excelled it in popularity and influence. The first edition of Thomas Bewick's *General History of Quadrupeds* (1790) included a modest engraving of an elk, and some half a dozen pages of description and comment. Unlike Johnson, Bewick was well aware that the moose and the elk – 'the largest and most formidable of the deer kind' – were one creature known by two names. Like Johnson, he was mildly sceptical about travellers' yarns, though not dogmatic: 'by some, it is said to be twelve feet high; while others, with greater appearance of probability, describe it as being not much higher than a Horse. It is, however, a matter of doubt to which a greater degree of credibility should be given.'[5]

Four decades later, John James Audubon and the Revd John Bachman, with the assistance of John James's sons John Woodhouse and Victor G., produced *The Viviparous Quadrupeds of North America*. Published between 1845 and 1848, it was by far the most ambitious attempt thus far to document the full range of North American mammal life. The younger Audubon's portrait of a 'Moose Deer', plate LXXVI, shows a standing bull and a recumbent cow with single calf. Sadly, it is rather a stilted, insipid portrait, and does not bear comparison with the bird

'The Elk', from Thomas Bewick's *A General History of Quadrupeds* (1790).

studies for which Audubon remains famous. At this period, the painters of the United States were outshone by its writers – particularly in the year 1853, the *annus mirabilis* of moose literature.

THE YEAR 1853: LOWELL AND THOREAU

'In the late summer of 1853,' wrote the American critic and editor Charles Shain, 'two leading members of the most illustrious generation of literary men New England has ever produced went to Maine in search of material. Each was on a visit to that special part of the New England territory, the Maine wilderness, and Maine's symbolic animal, the outlandish moose.'[6] James Russell Lowell came first, and arrived at Greenville on Moosehead Lake on 13 August. Henry David Thoreau arrived in Bangor almost exactly a month later, on 14 September; this was his second venture into the territory. As Shain points out, for the citified Lowell and other men of letters, Maine provided the New England equivalent of the Wild West, with moose in place of buffalo.

Both Lowell and Thoreau published articles about their adventures: Lowell published his in a recently established literary journal, *Putnam's*, published in New York; Thoreau's piece appeared in a Boston journal, also new, the *Atlantic Monthly*. (The editor of *Atlantic Monthly* was one James Russell Lowell.) Lowell wrote:

After paddling a couple of miles, we found the arbored mouth of the little Malahoodus River, famous for moose. We had been on the look-out for it, and I was amused to hear one of the hunters say to the other, to assure himself of his familiarity with the spot, 'You drove the West Branch last spring, didn't you?' as one of us might ask

On Stone by W E Hitchcock

A family of moose, from J. J. Audubon and Revd John Bachman's *The Viviparous Quadrupeds of North America* (1845–8).

about a horse. We did not explore the Malahoodus far, but left the other birch to thread its cedar solitudes, while we turned back to try our fortunes in the larger stream. We paddled on about four miles farther, lingering now and then opposite the black mouth of a moose-path . . .

Half past Eleven, P.M. – No sign of a moose yet . . .

Quarter to Twelve . . . The water in the birch is about three inches deep, but the dampness reaches nearly to the waist. I am obliged to remove the matches from the ground-floor of my trousers into the upper story of a breast-pocket. Meanwhile we are to sit immovable, – for fear of frightening the moose, – which induces cramps . . .

Half past Twelve, – A crashing is heard on the left bank. This is a moose in good earnest. We are besought to hold our breaths, if possible, My fingers so numb, I could not, if I tried. Crash! crash! again, and then a plunge, followed by a dead stillness. 'Swimmin' crik,' whispers guide, suppressing all unnecessary parts of speech, – 'don't stir.' I, for one, am not likely to. A cold fog which has been gathering for the last hour has finished me. I fancy myself one of those naked pigs that seem rushing out of market-doors in the winter, frozen in a ghastly attitude of gallop. If I were to be shot myself, I should feel no interest in it. As it is, I am only a spectator, having declined a gun. Splash! again; this time the moose is in

A moose from Etienne-Geoffroy Saint-Hilaire and Frédéric Cuvier's *Histoire naturelle des mammifères* (1820–42): a more accurate depiction than Audubon's.

sight, and click! click! one rifle misses fire after the other. The fog has quietly spiked our batteries. The moose goes on crashing up the bank, and presently we can hear it chewing its cud close by. So we lie in wait, freezing.

Their hunt was unsuccessful.

Literary history has not been kind to Lowell's reputation; he is now considered no more than a genteel minor ornament of American letters. Thoreau, by contrast, has been elevated to the rank of classic, thanks largely to the enduring appeal of *Walden*, his meditative account of a period of rural solitude and self-sufficiency.

If the wildlife painter Carl Rungius is the Rembrandt of the moose, then Thoreau is surely the Wordsworth. He is the only great writer to have taken the moose as one of his major subjects, and a reliable report states that his dying words were 'Moose . . . Indians . . . '. Thoreau's travel book, *The Maine Woods*, published posthumously in book form in 1864, is the only text of canonical stature to dwell at length on the creatures he memorably called 'God's own horses'. It includes a lengthy account of the day on which Thoreau, unarmed, went along as a participant observer on a moose hunt:

I heard a slight crackling of twigs deep in the alders and turned Joe's attention to it; whereupon he began to push the canoe back rapidly; and we had receded thus half a dozen rods, when we suddenly spied two moose standing just on the edge of the open part of the meadow which we had passed, not six or seven rods distant, looking round the alders at us. They made me think of great frightened rabbits, with their long ears and half-inquisitive, half-frightened looks; the true denizens of the forest, (I saw at once,) filling a vacuum which now first I discovered had not been filled for me, – 'moose'-men, 'wood-eaters,' the word is said to mean, – clad in a sort of Vermont gray, or homespun. Our Nimrod, owing to the retrograde movement, was now the furthest from the game, but being warned of its neighbourhood, he hastily stood up, and while we ducked, fired over our heads, one barrel at the foremost, which alone he saw, though he did not know what kind of creature it was; whereupon this one dashed across the meadow and up a high bank on the north-east, so rapidly as to leave but an indistinct impression of its outlines on my mind. At the same instant, the other, a young one, but as tall as a horse, leaped out into the stream, in full sight, and there stood cowering for a moment, or rather its disproportionate lowness behind gave it that appearance, and uttering two or three trumpeting squeaks. I have an indistinct recollection of seeing the old one pause an instant on the top of the bank in the woods, look towards its shivering young, and then dash away again. The second barrel was levelled at the calf, and when we expected to see it drop in the water, after a little hesitation, it too got out of the water, and dashed up the hill, though in a somewhat different direction.[7]

Part of his reaction was a sense of bafflement:

The moose is singularly grotesque and awkward to look at. Why should it stand so high at the shoulders? Why have so long a head? Why have no tail to speak of? for in my examination I overlooked it entirely. Naturalists say it is one inch and a half long. It reminded me at once of the cameleopard, high before and low behind . . . The moose will perhaps one day become extinct, but how naturally then, when it exists only as a fossil relic, and unseen as that, may the poet or sculptor invent a fabulous animal with similar branching or leaving horns – a sort of fucus or lichen in bone – to be the inhabitant of such a forest as this![8]

His most fundamental feeling, however, was of remorse:

But, on more accounts than one, I had had enough of moose-hunting. I had not come to the woods for this purpose, nor had I foreseen it, though I had been willing to learn how the Indian manoeuvred; but one moose killed was as good, if not as bad, as a dozen. The afternoon's tragedy, and my share in it, as it affected the innocence, destroyed the pleasure of my adventure. It is true, I came as near as is possible to come to being a hunter and miss it, as possible myself; and as it is, I think that I could spend a year in the woods, fishing and hunting just enough to sustain myself, with satisfaction. This would be next to living like a philosopher on the fruits of the earth which you had raised, which also attracts me. But this hunting of the moose merely for the satisfaction of killing him, – not even for the sake of his hide, – without making any extraordinary exertion or running any risk yourself, is too much like going out by night to some wood-side pasture and shooting your neighbour's horses. These are God's own horses, poor, timid creatures, that will run fast enough as soon as they smell you, though they *are* nine feet high . . .

Other white men and Indians who come here are hunters, whose object is to slay as many moose and other wild animals as possible. But, pray, could one not spend some weeks or years in the solitude of this vast wilderness with other employments than these – employments perfectly sweet and innocent and ennobling? For one that comes with a pencil to sketch or sing, a thousand come with an axe or rifle. What a coarse and imperfect use Indians and hunters make of nature! No wonder that their race is so soon exterminated. I, already, and for weeks afterward, felt my nature the coarser for this part of my woodland experience, and was reminded that our life should be lived as tenderly and daintily as one would pluck a flower.[9]

As early as 1856 Thoreau had noted in his *Journals* that two hundred years of European incursions had driven a number of

Moose in a lake, Innoko National Wildlife Refuge, Alaska. Moose do not thrive in warmer temperatures, and in summer months will seek out ponds, lakes and streams to lower their body temperature.

indigenous species to extinction in many areas. 'When I consider that the nobler animals have been eliminated here, – the cougar, panther, lynx, wolverine, wolf, bear, moose, deer, the beaver, the turkey, etc., etc., – I cannot [but] feel as if I lived in a tamed and, as it were, emasculated country.'[10]

Thoreau is sometimes spoken of as a kind of prophet; and his lament for the passing of American wildlife anticipates many other writers on moose, particularly those of the half-century or so after his death, when it seemed to many reflective souls that the moose was doomed.

THE IRISH ELK

As we have seen, when reports of a large quadruped with extremely dramatic, palmate antlers began to filter back across the Atlantic, a number of scholars – notably Dr Thomas Molyneux, in an essay of 1697 – asked themselves whether this new-found beast might provide the answer to a riddle that had been perplexing savants for decades. Was the 'moose', this bizarre creature mentioned in doubtfully accurate reports from North America, in fact the living relative of an enigmatic, stag-like animal from past times, blessed with astonishingly huge antlers and known (because at this point its fossil remains had been found only in Ireland) as the Irish elk?

It was not, though the debate was not clarified until the time of Georges Cuvier, and in some details not fully settled until the twentieth century. For most of the eighteenth century, learned opinion was about equally divided between those who held that the Irish elk was indeed a type of moose and their opponents, who supported a reindeer theory. The late evolutionary biologist and wit Stephen Jay Gould told the long story crisply and amusingly in his essay on 'The Misnamed,

A 19th-century engraving of the skeleton of a Great Irish elk in the Royal Museum, Edinburgh, with a human skeleton to indicate scale.

Mistreated, and Misunderstood Irish Elk'. Gould makes the Irish elk a conceptual peer of the Holy Roman Empire (which, as Voltaire was one of the first to point out, was neither holy, nor Roman, nor an empire) and the English horn (which is a Continental oboe, 'English' being a corruption of various adjectives meaning 'angular'). The Irish elk was not an elk at all, but a deer – its closest surviving relative is usually held to be the fallow deer – and its habitat was not exclusively Irish.

The latter reality, at least, began to dawn in the mid-eighteenth century, after 'Irish' elk remains were found in Yorkshire in 1746. More 'Elk' fossils were unearthed in Germany in 1781, and the first complete skeleton was discovered on the Isle of Man in the 1820s. Subsequent investigations established that the Irish elk had ranged as far east as China and as far south as North Africa.

Why was the issue so anxiously debated? The answer concerns religion rather than biology, as we understand it: among the pious natural philosophers of the seventeenth century, there was a consensus that for any species to become quite extinct would contradict God's infinite goodness and mercy. Molyneux put it thus:

> That no real species of living creatures is so utterly extinct, as to be lost entirely out of the World, since it was first created, is the opinion of many naturalists; and 'tis grounded on so good a principle of Providence taking care in general of all its animal productions, that it deserves our assent.

And yet no one had ever encountered a living Irish elk. So for Molyneux and his like, the moose was an answer to their prayers for a sign: a breathing, eating, ruminating proof of God's perfection as Creator. Molyneux, it should be added, never actually encountered a moose, even in skeletal form, and was relying on travellers' accounts. He concluded, to his own peace of mind, that the Irish elk had died out only in Ireland – his conjecture was that the breed succumbed to an 'epidemick distemper' caused by 'a certain ill constitution of air' – and that it continued to thrive in the forests across the Atlantic.

This was not, at the time, an unreasonable conjecture, but as the rapidly developing earth sciences of the eighteenth century turned up more and more fossil remains, it became harder and harder for those who were thoughtful as well as pious to deny that not just one or two, but countless species had lost the fierce contest for life, and left nothing behind but a few traces in the rocks. By 1812 a French palaeontologist had drawn up a minute analysis of the Irish elk remains that proved that the beast was not like any of its plausible modern counterparts;

and, by comparing it with the remains of other extinct species, he had begun the task of dating the period of extinction.

Though it remained possible for some Christians to maintain that the Irish elk had for some reason not been invited onto Noah's Ark, and had thus perished in the Flood, the idea of extinction – or even multiple extinctions – was slowly becoming a cornerstone of educated opinion. The question now was not whether the Irish elk had undergone extinction, but by what means, and when? One Archdeacon Maunsell, in 1825, wrote that he 'apprehended they must have been destroyed by some overwhelming deluge'. The next candidate for the most likely means of destruction was *Homo sapiens*. 'Sir Thomas Molyneux conceived that a sort of distemper, or pestilential murrain, might have cut off the Irish Elks', wrote a Mr Hibbert in 1830. 'It is, however, questionable, if the human race has not occasionally proved as formidable as the pestilence in exterminating from various districts, whole races of wild animals.'

Fortunately for the good name of our species, the British palaeontologist Sir Richard Owen reviewed the evidence and showed that the giant deer had perished in Ireland long before men had settled there. At the end of the following decade, in 1859, Darwin published *The Origin of Species*, and the terms of debate changed yet again. Darwin's case was so powerful that those who wished to argue with him on his own terms, rather than simply calling on dogma, would be obliged to find instances where his theory of natural selection did not hold true. If the anti-Darwinians could show that in some cases evolution had simply proceeded in straight lines that could not be stopped, even if they led to extinction, then the Darwinian theory could be shown to be seriously leaky.

Anti-Darwinians called their opposing theory 'orthogenesis', and the case of the Irish elk was crucial to it. Why, the orthogeneticists asked once again, had the Irish elk died? And the answer this time was that it was doomed by its greatest asset. The magnificent weapons on their brows eventually grew so large – estimates of 12 feet (3.7 m) across were held to be reasonable – that they literally dragged the poor brutes down head-first, so that they drowned in swamps, were trapped in branches, or simply pulled to the ground.

It seemed like a pretty good objection, and it was repeated in the enemy camp until the 1930s, when Julian Huxley and others launched a devastating counter-attack. Central to Huxley's argument was the concept of 'allometry', the study of the relationship between shape and size. In simple terms, he had noted that, as deer grow larger, their antlers do not grow at the same rate as their bodies, but faster, so that the antlers of a big deer are both absolutely and relatively larger than those of small deer. Since the Irish elk was the largest of all known deer, it was entirely within Darwinian logic that their antlers should be enormous. By focusing on the antlers alone, the orthogeneticists had overlooked the absolute evolutionary advantage of a larger body size. Game, set and match to the Darwinians?

Well, almost. It fell to Gould himself to spot the fact that wonderful refutation, repeated in generations of textbooks (is there perhaps something Darwinian about this survival itself?), was based on no direct observation whatsoever. Huxley and Co. had indeed examined deer, but no one had bothered to go and measure the fossil remains to see if the antler growth principle had been as true for extinct deer as for living ones. To condense the story, Gould took himself to Adare Manor, home of the Earl of Dunraven, and set to work. Sure enough, the allometric principle held true once again.

But Gould remained unsatisfied, feeling that the Huxley position – that huge antlers were, so to speak, tolerated by natural selection rather than governed by it – silently ceded too much ground to the orthogeneticists. 'The opposite interpretation is equally possible: that selection operated primarily to increase antler size, thus yielding increased body size as a secondary consequence.' Gould turned from the pages of *Origin of Species* to Darwin's later work, *The Descent of Man* (1871), in which Darwin toys for a while with the possibility that elk antlers, far from being lethal weapons, are primarily ornaments to attract females.

This was a brilliant leap of intellect. Modern studies of animals have proved that in many cases, the bodily structures once assumed to be serious weapons of combat are indeed used in predominantly ritual ways, to prevent actual battle by establishing clear, if frequently contested, hierarchies among males of breeding age. Large antlers attract lady elks. And in the case of the Irish elk, where the palms of the antlers are arranged so as to face forwards for major visual impact when the male is looking straight ahead, the likelihood that they were used for display rather than duelling becomes all the greater.

So what, finally, did wipe out the Irish elk? The best answer to this is the same thing that is likely to do for our species unless we look sharp: climate change. Irish elk thrived in a brief warm spell of about a thousand years, which took place roughly 12,000 to 11,000 years ago. When the temperatures dropped, so did the elk.

5 The Symbolic Moose

It is largely in the later nineteenth century that we see the transition from the primarily observational representations of moose – practical, scientific, classificatory or utilitarian (the tradition, that is, of Bewick and Heriot) – to the fine art (or, more often, the popular equivalent of fine art) conventions of drama, anecdote, nostalgia, pathos and uplift. In short, the period from the nineteenth century to the early twentieth is that in which the moose becomes increasingly emblematic, allegorical or anthropomorphized.

From 1857 to 1907 the firm of Currier & Ives, New York, mass produced coloured lithographic prints as inexpensive items of decoration – some 7,000 images in all, in huge editions. Depicting mainly scenes of American history and wildlife, these embraced most flavours of popular sentimentality from the melodramatic to the idyllic, and moose – quintessentially American, or so it seemed to householders – were among the more saleable images. Currier & Ives art was often more striking for its drama than its zoological accuracy; for example, the 'moose' represented in *Moose and Wolves* (see over) is a strange composite beast with the shoulders and head of a cow bison and the pointed antlers of a wapiti. Frederick Remington, one of the most commercially successful artists of his day, is best remembered for his studies of the American West, but he too turned his

THE MOOSE DEER OR ELK.
In the Garden of the Zoological Society

attention to moose: see, among others, *A Moose Bull Fight* of 1890. Besides Remington, the leading American moose artists of the period were Proctor, Rungius and Shiras.

Alexander Phiminster Proctor (1862–1950) was commissioned to sculpt 37 life-sized American wilderness animals for the World's Columbia Exposition in Chicago in 1893 (and thus one year late for the precise tetracentenary of Columbus's expedition of 1492). More than 20 million Americans visited the 'City of Palaces', built at a cost of $28 million on the shore of Lake Michigan. To enter its Administration Building from the South Lagoon, they would first have to cross a bridge, the eastern entrance to which was flanked by two splendid Proctor moose. As Franzmann remarks, the United States was now such

The Moose Deer or Elk, a hand-coloured 19th-century engraving.

Few city-dwelling Americans in the 19th century who bought popular prints by Currier & Ives such as this dramatic scene, *Moose and Wolves: A Narrow Escape*, would have seen a moose in the wild – a fact that allowed artists to be very fanciful in their depictions. This 'moose' looks more like a cross between a bison and a wapiti.

an urban nation that this would be the closest the vast majority of Americans would ever come to meeting a moose face to face.

The German-born wildlife artist Carl Rungius (1869–1959) has been called 'the Rembrandt of the Moose'. Once, when asked to name his favourite subject, he replied 'Mooses in spruces'. He first visited the United States in 1894; soon afterwards, he went hunting in Maine, but failed to bag a moose. Had he taken a moose, his family thought, he might have returned happily to Germany. But his soul was discontented. An uncle gave him the money to return the following year, and his fascination for American wildlife waxed as he turned from slaughtering beasts to immortalizing them. His biographers speculate that his fascination for the moose was that they 'symbolised for Europeans the spirit of wilderness'. Quite so, but this was hardly the case for Europeans alone.

George Shiras III of Pennsylvania was eminent in three fields, as a politician, conservationist and wildlife photographer. As a Congressman, he had drafted a bill that was the first official recognition of the Federal government's duty to protect and preserve migratory birds; this became the foundation for the Weeks-McLean bill enacted in 1913, as well as for the migratory bird treaty signed between the United States and Canada in 1916. But it was in his less official capacity as a propagandist for the cause of conservation in general that he had the most lasting influence, and a good deal of his persuasive power was due to the excellent wildlife photographs he shot and published.

Though concerned with the fate of all species, Shiras was particularly fascinated by moose; he photographed them regularly, and was the first photographer ever to manage to take a night-flash portrait of the shy creature. Paddling his canoe, he quietly approached a cow moose that was grazing along the shoreline; he paused, set up his camera, and ignited the flash. Startled, the cow sought refuge in the water, and almost capsized his canoe. Shiras's camera fell overboard, but he managed to recover it with the exposed plate intact.

Elsewhere, he described his adventures while photographing moose in the Kenai Peninsula. On one occasion, he attempted to take a shot of an elderly cow moose at a mud-hole:

Determined to try for a close picture, and to test her disposition when thus interrupted, I boldly walked in view, crossing the bare and much-trampled field to within fifty feet. She stood broadside, head up, and unquestionably looking at me out of one eye, but to all appearances utterly indifferent to my approach. Taking a picture, I went a little closer, when she turned away without looking, and again the camera recorded the scene.

While changing plate-holders, I was surprised to see the moose turn about and come toward me on a slow trot. To the uninitiated this would probably have meant a bold charge, and to the nature faker sufficient cause for an exciting story . . . Wishing to avoid alarming her so soon, I backed across the field to the edge of the marsh, but she still followed. Turning my back to the animal, I walked ahead, and upon reaching a place where the ground was almost impassible with fallen timber, I stopped . . . the cow immediately came up, circled almost within reach, and then was struck by the scent. The effect was instantaneous and remarkable . . . With a quick awkward plunge, she made off at her fastest gait.[1]

He published dozens of his moose studies in *National Geographic Magazine*, and later in the two-volume *Hunting Wildlife with Camera and Flashlight*, which contained no fewer than 65 images of moose. Now that the United States had become an urban, industrial nation, these were, as Franzmann notes, the first true images of moose that most Americans had ever seen. Shiras's care for moose won him a measure of immortality – his friend Edward W. Nelson of the US Bureau of Biological Survey called the sub-species found in the Rockies 'Shira's [*sic*] Moose' – also known as the Yellowstone moose or the Wyoming moose, *Alces alces shirasi*.

As artistic portrayals of moose grew more popular, so did the practice of using the beast as an emblem – in heraldry, in commerce, in the armed forces of various nations and in popular culture. The practice had begun early, with the Hudson's Bay Company. For almost three centuries, the company's coat of arms perpetuated the moose/elk confusion, since the College of Heralds, instructed by the HBC to show two rampant 'elk' – that is, moose – supporting a shield showing four beavers and a fox above a crown, assumed that a North American elk was intended. (*Pro pelle cutem*, the HBC motto, is commonly translated as

The heraldic arms of the Hudson's Bay Company. For many years, thanks to the familiar confusion between the European elk (moose) and the North American elk (wapiti), this achievement mistakenly incorporated wapiti. Wags inside the Company said that the Latin motto should be translated as 'Properly cut 'em'.

'A Skin for a Skin', though wags within the HBC claimed that it meant 'Properly cut 'em.'²) The error was finally corrected in the twentieth century – as early as 1927, according to records of the company seal over Beaver House – and from 1962 onwards the shield supporters became the moose that were always intended.

Where the Hudson's Bay Company blazed an emblematic trail, others followed. In the US, moose adorn the state seals of Michigan and Maine; in the latter, the creature is shown curled up at the base of a pine tree. In Canada, the provincial coat of arms of Ontario is flanked to the left by a moose and the right by a wapiti. Many Canadian bodies have also used the moose to signal their identity (one, mildly derisive American slang term

Insignia for the Canadian naval vessel HMCS *Moose*.

Insignia for 419 Squadron, Royal Canadian Air Force.

Insignia for the Tribal Police, Kongiganak, Alaska.

for Canadians is 'moose-huggers'[3]). Two squadrons of the Royal Canadian Air Force that participated in the Battle of Britain adopted a moose head as the central element of their insignia: No. 242 squadron and No. 419 squadron. The latter owed its name to its first commanding officer, Wing Commander John 'Moose' Fulton, from Kamloops, British Columbia. Beneath the image of an aggressive bull moose in profile runs the motto *Emoosa Aswayita*: 'Beware of the Moose' in Cree. The fifteenth wing of the Canadian Air Force, stationed at Moose Jaw, Saskatchewan, has also adopted a moose as its squadron badge;

Insignia for the international friendly society and charity, the Loyal Order of Moose.

and there are many, many further examples of moose emblems in other branches of the Canadian and United States armed forces and police departments.

In this context, it would be churlish not to mention the benevolent and social organization – one of the largest in the world – today known as Moose International or International Order of Moose, with its female auxiliary outfit, Women of the Moose. (MI was formerly known as the Loyal Order of Moose.) Today, the MI can boast some 1.8 million members, organized into 2,300 Moose Lodges and directed from its headquarters in Mooseheart, Illinois. According to one of its leading members, K. N. Wehrmeister, the reason for having chosen the moose as totemic animal was admiration for its ethical qualities:

> Strong and majestic, the moose is unique in all the animal kingdom . . . He takes only what he needs, nothing more. He loves freedom and is the master of his domain. Yet for his great size and strength he lives in peace with other creatures. The moose uses his size and power not to

An Alaskan moose with admirers, c. 1900–1930.

dominate but to protect, not to spoil but to preserve. He is a fierce protector, a loyal companion, and a generous provider who brings comfort and security to those within his vision.[4]

Honorary members of the Loyal Order of Moose have included several presidents: Warren G. Harding, Franklin D. Roosevelt, Harry S. Truman and, most apt for our purposes, Theodore Roosevelt, also founder of the Bull Moose Party.

THE BULL MOOSE PARTY

Theodore Roosevelt, twenty-sixth president of the United States, is at least as famous for his wildlife exploits – first as hunter, then as conservationist – as for his many and remarkable political and military accomplishments. A whirlwind of nervous energy, he used some of his rare free time to write more than 30 books, seven of them dedicated to his hunting exploits. During his stay in the White House, he decorated the State Dining Room with mounted trophies of the animals he had shot; pride of place, over the main fireplace, was given to the stuffed head of a bull moose.

His first successful moose hunt was in the Bitterroot Mountains, on the Montana/Idaho border, in 1887. As he remembered it some years later:

At last we reached the hummock, and I got into position for a shot, taking a final look at my faithful 45–90 Winchester to see that all was in order. Peering cautiously through the shielding evergreens, I at first could not make out where the moose was lying, until my eye was caught by the motion of his big ears, as he occasionally flapped them lazily forward. Even then I could not see his outline; but I knew where he was, and having pushed my rifle forward on the moss, I snapped a dry twig to make him rise. My veins were thrilling and my heart beating with that eager, fierce excitement, known only to the hunter of big game, and forming one of the keenest and strongest pleasures which with him go to make up 'the wild joy of living'. As the sound of the snapping twig smote his ears the moose rose nimbly to his feet, with a lightness on which one would not have reckoned in a beast so heavy in body. He stood broadside to me for a moment, his ungainly head slightly turned, while his ears twitched and his nostrils sniffed the air. Drawing a fine bead against his back hide, behind his shoulder and two thirds his body's depth below his shaggy withers, I pressed the trigger . . . [5]

Another moose hunt, on 19 September 1915:

When we turned he followed us back, and thus went to and fro with us. Where the water was deep near shore, we pushed the canoe close in to him, and he promptly rushed down to the water's edge, shaking his head, and striking the earth with his fore hoofs. We shouted at him but with no effect . . . Altogether the huge black beast looked like a formidable customer, and was evidently in a most evil rage and bent on man-killing. For over an hour he thus kept us from the shore, running to meet us wherever we tried to go.

Eventually, Roosevelt continues, the moose seemed to tire of its campaign, and went off along the route of a stream that ran parallel with the trail that the canoe party would have to take to reach their base camp. After waiting for a few minutes in silence, they decided that the creature had gone and that it was safe to proceed.

A couple of hundred yards on, the trail led to within a few yards of the little river. As we reached this point a smashing in the brush beyond the opposite bank caused us to wheel, and the great bull came headlong for us, while Arthur called to me to shoot. With a last hope of frightening him I fired over his head, without the slightest effect. At a slashing trot he crossed the river, shaking his head, his ears back, the hair on his withers bristling.

'Tirez, m'sieu, tirez! vite, vite!' called Arthur; and when the bull was not thirty feet off I put a bullet into his

'Bully!', a cartoon from the *Cleveland Plain Dealer*, 9 August 1912, showing Senator Theodore Roosevelt as a were-moose, being courted by different regional interests. 'Bully!' was one of Roosevelt's favourite expressions of enthusiasm.

chest, in the sticking point. It was a mortal wound and
stopped him short.

I do not believe that this vicious bull moose had ever
seen a man. I have never heard of another moose acting
with the same determination and perseverance in fero-
cious malice; it behaved, as I have said, like some of the
rare vicious rogues among African elephants, buffaloes,
and rhinoceroses.[6]

Roosevelt served two terms as president, from 1901 to 1909,
then initially supported William Howard Taft to replace him as
Republican party leader. But he soon grew dissatisfied with
Taft, and quit the Republicans to seek a third term in office as
the nominee of the Progressive Party, soon known to all as the
'Bull Moose' party. The party was short-lived – just four years,
from 1912 to 1916 – but has endured in popular memory to a
surprising degree. One of the publicity stunts devised for the
election campaign was a gimmick photo, which showed Roosevelt apparently riding a moose as it swam down a river. Only the

very unsophisticated were fooled, but the image reinforced Roosevelt's popular image as an outdoorsy man of pluck and grit. That image was given an unexpected boost by a failed assassination attempt on Roosevelt in Milwaukee, Wisconsin, on 14 October 1912. Roosevelt was shot point-blank in the chest by his would-be killer, but his wounds were extraordinarily slight – thanks, it later proved, to a wedge of rolled-up paper (his speech) and a metal spectacle case through which the assassin's bullet had passed before piercing his chest. Making the most of his almost supernatural-looking endurance, Roosevelt triumphantly declared to the crowd: 'It takes more than that to kill a Bull Moose!' (As early as 1900, he had boasted 'I am as strong as a Bull Moose!')

Another element of Bull Moose campaigning was some doggerel by one Arthur Guiterman:

> The Bull Moose is galloping over the world
> And he loudly refuses to do as he's told.
> He tosses his antlers and goes it alone;
> For he scorns all conventions – excepting his own.[7]

Today, the term 'bull moose' is occasionally applied to a politician from the East Coast who travels west to boost his spirit – or his popularity in those parts – before standing for election.

MOOSE TALES

As real-life moose populations dwindled before the hunters' rifles, fictional moose proliferated, in such juvenile novels as W. A. Fraser's *Moosewa* (1900) and Clarence Hawkes's *Shovelhorns* (1909). Older readers also began to show a taste for tales of moose life, and were served by the likes of Agnes

Herbert's *The Moose* of 1913. Its prose tends frequently to the purple, lightly seasoned with the twee, and the vocabulary would be quite demanding for very young readers:

> One by one the stars, marguerites in a sea of ultra-marine, went out, and little filmy clouds, crimson and rose, golden and blue, banked the horizon. In the transparency of the atmosphere the trees, in fretted silhouette, stood gaunt and desolate, and down the trail the vaporous night mists tiptoed before the wind swinging down from the ice-bound mountain-tops.

THE MOOSE

AGNES HERBERT

The story, however, is entirely straightforward, and follows eleven years in the life of Moosewa (the author explains that this is a Cree word meaning 'wood-eater'), from his infancy to his death by drowning. Like Bambi, Moosewa loses his mother to a hunter's shot at a very early age, and is captured by a trapper as a pet for his woman, Sadie. Pampered by Sadie, tortured and branded by the men, Moosewa eventually escapes and attaches himself to a bull moose mentor, until it is time for him to declare his adulthood, claim a cow (in the first instance, a much older female, beyond her fertile years), and eventually grow into the most magnificent moose in Alaska.

Herbert anthropomorphizes freely about the 'forest folk' and their culture – all the animals believe that beavers created the world – but much of her biology is surprisingly reliable, and she makes no attempt to pretend, for example, that a male moose would feel any enduring loyalty to its mates. About humans she is largely scathing, particularly if they are Chinese, but she respects the harshness of the trappers' lives and hints to the reader not to feel too outraged at, for example, the spectacle of bear cubs being battered to death. 'Those that are without a muff among you cast the first stone.'[8] Despite these redeeming features, there is little in Herbert's work that might diminish the reputations of Kipling or Kenneth Grahame. When it comes to the depiction of moose, non-fiction accounts are generally the best.

One of the most significant of such non-fiction writers, Ernest Thompson Seton, was both an artist and a naturalist, prolific in both fields. Today he is most frequently remembered as the co-founder of the American Boy Scouts' movement. He wrote about many species, especially those that he hunted for sport rather than portraiture, and one of his classic accounts of

Locked moose antlers, from Ernest Thompson Seton's *Lives of Game Animals* (1924–8).

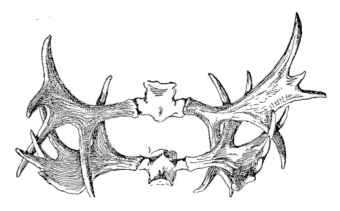

moose may be found in *Life-Histories of Northern Animals* (1909).

Only once did Seton go on a moose-hunt, and he describes his experiences in *Trail of an Artist-Naturalist* (1940), where he devotes an entire chapter to the event. The hunt took place near Carberry, Manitoba, in October 1884, lasted nineteen days of stalking through snow, and covered well over 300 miles. Eventually he fired some wounding shots into his quarry:

> With feelings of mingled hope and fear we crossed over to his trail; and there – oh, savage glee! At every stride was a jet of blood. What a thrill of hope and triumph!
>
> 'Our moose, Jim, if I have to follow it to Brandon!'
>
> 'Not so far as that,' said Jim, pointing to the crimson streaks.
>
> And away we ran on the trail like wolves, fairly gloating over the continued jets of blood.
>
> I had read so much of the tremendous distances that a moose will travel, even with a mortal wound, that I was prepared for a ten-mile run: but, to my surprise, before we had gone four hundred yards, Jim shouted 'Here he is!'
>
> Sure enough, there he lay, with his knees doubled under him, like an ox in pasture. As we drew near, he looked back calmly over his shoulder.
>
> 'Guess we better bleed him,' said Jim.
>
> 'Guess you better look out,' said I. 'I'd as soon go near a wounded lion.'
>
> 'Well, let's give him a couple more balls.'
>
> So we both fired into him – without the slightest visible effect.
>
> 'Let's go round to his head.'

Accordingly, we went around, keeping at a safe distance. Jim was about to fire when our victim's head drooped, then fell flat. I put a ball through his brain. His leg straightened out, he quivered, and lay still. The moose was dead.

Jim bled him. Then we stood for a few minutes, gazing on the magnificent beast, with feelings of rapture and triumph.[9]

Male elk, from Richard Lydekker's *The Deer of All Lands* (1898).

A hunting scene, from Theo Johnson's *Wild Animals: Mammals* (1891).

But the rapture is short-lived. Seton's dream to one day bag 'the grandest beast that roams America's woods' sours when he looks at the hacked-up remains of a large bull 'turned into a pile of butcher's meat, for the sake of a passing thrill of triumph . . . [I] then and there made a vow, which I have lived up to ever since – that so long as they are threatened with early extinction, I will never again lift my rifle against any of America's big game.'[10]

As the century drew to a close, many voices joined the chorus of lamentation that had been begun by Thoreau. In 1876 Windham Wyndham-Quin, 4th Earl of Dunraven, wrote:

The method of butchering a moose: from an article written and illustrated by Frederick Remington for *Harper's New Monthly Magazine* (1899).

137

Poor *Cervus Alces*! your ungainly form has an old-time look about it; your very appearance seems out of keeping with the present day. The smoke of the chimney, the sound of the axe, are surely though slowly encroaching on your wild domains. The atmosphere of civilization is death to you, and in spite of your exquisitely keen senses of smell and hearing, you too will soon have to be placed in the category of things that have been.[11]

And in 1894 Madison Grant noted that moose 'shrink back before the most advanced outpost of civilization, and soon vanish altogether, leaving behind the names of lakes, rivers, and mountains as the only evidence of their existence'.[12]

As the nineteenth century gave way to the twentieth, the future for moose looked bleak.

6 The Modern Moose

Eins within a space and a wearywide space it wast ere
wohned a Mookse. The onesomeness wast alltolonely,
archunsitslike, broady oval, and a Mookse he would a walking go
James Joyce, *Finnegans Wake* (1939)

Of all the wonders of nature, a tree in summer is perhaps the
most remarkable; with the possible exception of a moose
singing 'Embraceable You' in spats.
Woody Allen

The threatened extinction, which to many troubled observers
in the years leading up to 1900 seemed at best a few bloody and
remorseless hunting seasons away, never happened. On the
contrary. A range of new hunting laws and other conservation
measures – not least, the creation of federally controlled
national parks and game preserves – put an end to the slaughter,
and moose numbers soon began to grow again, and were already
beginning to reach quite healthy levels by the 1920s. Moreover,
moose began to spread well beyond their previous ranges in
North America, occupying territories in which they had previ-
ously been unknown.

Legal protection for moose began in Maine in 1883. In 1897
the Federal Government had 50 moose under its protection
in Yellowstone Park; by 1912 their numbers had, according to
official reports, increased to at least 550, but private estimates
put the figure much higher, at some 1,500. Moose have been
legally protected in Michigan since 1889. Writing in 1910,
Ernest Thompson Seton made a rough calculation. 'The entire
[American] range of the moose is about 3,500,000 square miles',
he proposed, so that 'at a very rough estimate, we may put the
whole range at a round million of moose.' The numbers of

Katie Cuddon,
*Outcast (Female
Moose)*, 2007, oil
on ceramic.

European moose at the same time were estimated at about twice that figure, which gives a total world population in the early twentieth century of about three million.

Not all the conservation measures were successful. An attempt in 1902 to reintroduce moose to the Adirondacks – by releasing seven or eight adults which had been caught in Canada – ended ignominiously. Some were mistaken, or 'mistaken' for deer and shot; the others disappeared, presumably having found their way back to Canada. The bill for the whole enterprise was US$3,000. There was also a failed attempt to introduce moose to New Zealand. In January 1900 fourteen young specimens,

The memento of a record-breaking moose kill in Alaska, *c.* 1887; the animal's rack was some 69 inches (1.75m) wide.

procured from the HBC in British Columbia, were loaded on board a steamer bound from Vancouver. They soon encountered a severe storm, which killed ten of them, leaving two cows and two bulls as survivors.

On landing in Wellington, they were judged to be in good health, and were then liberated in Hokitaka Valley, on the west coast of South Island. For a few months, they remained more or less where they were left; then two bulls and one cow disappeared into dense forest, never to be seen again. The remaining cow, very tame, lived on near the settlement for the last fourteen years of her life. A second attempt was made in 1909–10, when

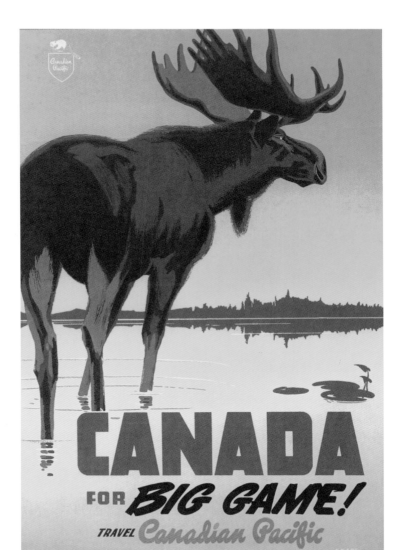

four young bulls and six cows were picked up in Banff, freighted via Fiji and Australia, and eventually released in the Fiordland National Park. This plan, too, appears to have failed.

Today, the North American region with the most substantial moose population is British Columbia, with an estimated 175,000 or more moose. The Canadian runner-up is New-foundland, with some 111,000. Alaska has an estimated 150,000 moose, spread across a very wide range. Maine, which comes second in the United States, has only about 29,000 moose, but is generally thought to have the highest population density of all the states. Outside the United States, Sweden is the modern nation with most moose – an estimated 200,000 to 250,000 each winter migration. The Swedish tourist industry exploits both the image and reality of moose: there is a moose farm not far from Stockholm, and at the end of 2007 a local authority in the north of the country announced its plans to build

A poster for Canadian Pacific Railway, c. 1950.

A moose frozen in ice after having attempted to swim across a lake in Sweden, 2003.

a major new attraction – a giant wooden moose, some 400 feet (122 m) long, containing a restaurant, a concert hall and other amenities.

Despite all the curiosity aroused by moose in laymen and learned alike, proper scientific study of the species came extraordinarily late. The taxidermist John Rowley constructed and installed the first moose exhibit at the American Museum of Natural History in New York around the turn of the century, but it was not until 1955 that Randolph L. Peterson published his book-length study *North American Moose* – still often cited as definitive, though his account of sub-species classifications has been questioned by more recent zoologists.[1] Peterson notes in his Introduction that the first extensive and scientifically rigorous essay on moose was published just two decades earlier, in 1934: Adolph Murie, 'The Moose of Isle Royale'. Isle Royale is a 47-mile-long island in Lake Superior, close to the Canadian shore. It was colonized by moose about 1910, and has now been studied longer than any other predator/prey system in the United States.[2]

Before Murie's work, Peterson contended, the field of moose studies had been dogged by gentlemanly amateurism. The account of moose biology established by Audubon and Bachman and Powell had, Peterson said, often been uncritically repeated by later authors, notably those with which we are already familiar: Major W. Ross King (*The Sportsman and Naturalist in Canada*, 1866), Madison Grant (*Moose*, 1902), W. T. Hornaday (*The American Natural History*, 1904) and, as we have seen, the widely read Ernest Thompson Seton (*Lives of Game Animals*, 1927).

Later in his career, Adolph Murie began to write essays on wildlife for a more general audience. His popular collection *A Naturalist in Alaska* was first published in 1961. Chapter Nine is wholly devoted to, as he puts it, the 'Picturesque Moose'; though his initial evocation of the beast is anything but picturesque, and belongs in the tradition of those nature writers who have found the moose rather unprepossessing.

> In the distance the moose looms as a huge, black animal wearing white stockings on rear legs. One's first impression may be that it is rather ungainly. And a close-up portrait of a cow-moose face would win no beauty contest, especially if she has just raised her head after submerging for water plants, with ears hanging and water dribbling from all points. The nose is long, bulbous, loose, and overhangs; the eyes are small, the ears long; the shoulder hump is exaggerated, and the legs are inordinately long.[3]

Yet to the eye of the evolutionary biologist, Murie goes on to explain, each of these ungainly features takes on a beauty of its own, for each plays its small part in the grand purpose of survival.

Murie goes on to reminisce about his period of moose-watching in Isle Royale, where he had the chance to spy on the animals in their mating season.

> For a number of evenings I stationed myself in an aspen or spruce tree at the head of one of the coves to observe activities. A cow would usually make her appearance at a salt lick, followed by a bull big enough to fight off all rivals. During the evening other grunting bulls could be heard in various directions. Young bulls were tolerated to some extent, but a large bull was a challenge. The bull in charge would advance toward a challenger with slow and measured step, grunting at intervals and stopping a few times to thrash the alder brush with his antlers or to demolish a sedge hummock. The approaching bull could also

be heard fighting brush and grunting. But the challenger always retreated from the bull in charge. At this time I found it easy to bring a bull to me by breaking branches or by uttering the wailing call of the cow. I often enticed bulls in this way almost to the foot of the tree from which I watched. On a few occasions a bull approached me in the woods, apparently hoping that the sounds of my walking came from an unattached female.[4]

It was not until well into the twentieth century, either, that scientists began to experiment with the possibility of taming moose. A wealth of anecdotal evidence as to the tractability of the beast soon found scientific confirmation. As Valerius Geist notes, 'when raised in captivity by caring human hands, moose emerge as affectionate, utterly loyal, brainy pets, more like huge, clever, mischievous dogs than like deer'.[5] Why, Geist asks himself, has mankind not devoted more attention to cultivating this agreeable beast after the manner of horses and dogs? His conclusion is that the moose is too demanding in its feeding habits, and too susceptible to livestock diseases.

Today, the leading centres of scientific research into moose are to be found in Alaska and Russia.

THE HUNTING REVIVAL

As we have seen, however troubled the history of the American conservation movement, it has at least one major triumph to its credit: 'the recovery of moose through most of its prehistoric North American range'.[6] In some states, notably Maine, the population density is now such that a serious hazard may often be posed by moose – vehicle collisions. As the moose returned in considerable numbers, various states felt free either to rein-

The aftermath of
a moose/car
collision in Alaska.

troduce legal hunting seasons or in some cases licensed hunting
for the first time: Utah permitted hunting of moose in 1950,
Minnesota in 1971, North Dakota in 1977, Washington and
Maine in 1980, Colorado in 1985, New Hampshire in 1988 and
Vermont in 1993.[7]

Hunting a moose with a high-powered modern rifle rather
than bow and arrow can seem like a contemptible occupation
even to those who otherwise endorse field sports. As one Maine
sportsman put it to me: 'you might as well go out and shoot
beer trucks' – meaning that the average moose target is so big
and so static that it would usually be harder to miss than hit
the creature. Still, for many hunters the lack of atavistic thrill
in modern moose-hunting is irrelevant. Many poorer families
in northern regions still depend on moose meat for a substantial part of their protein intake; and modern families
often find moose meat every bit as delicious as did Native
Americans of earlier centuries. Such hunts are, to be sure, not
without their critics.

Even today, there remain plenty of people in remote places for whom the flesh of moose is, if not quite the staff of life, then one of its greatest sweeteners:

> It is almost an axiom of human existence that what we desire most is scarce or difficult to obtain. And so it was with moose for the Koyukon people until a few decades past. This large animal, with its savory meat and treasured hide, was so rare that long journeys and persistent hunting were required to find it. But then the moose gradually increased to a point of real abundance in the Koyukuk wildlands, and it has remained common ever since.

Thus Richard K. Nelson, in his ethnographic essay-cum-travel memoir *Make Prayers to the Raven: A Koyukon View of the Northern Forest* of 1983. Nelson spent about sixteen months in the late 1970s doing fieldwork in the village of Huslia – about 250 miles from Fairbanks, Alaska, as the small plane flies. His hosts, the Koyukon Indians, are members of a nation that lives across a huge expanse of mostly wild country in northwestern interior Alaska, both north and south of the Arctic Circle.

As Nelson explains, there is conclusive evidence that moose were quite unknown in the valley region until about 1900; hunters would have to venture up-river to the territory known nowadays as Bettles, and then strike out on foot for the Ray Mountains and the Yukon drainage. They would often track the beasts for days at a time, walking with snowshoes. Even if they made a kill, they could only manage to bring the hide and a relatively small portion of meat back to their homes.

Gradually, an increase in moose numbers prompted the

animals to move within closer range. From the 1930s onwards the population thrived, reaching a plateau in the 1960s, and then began to decline again. Well aware of the precariousness of this resource, the hunters are concerned not to kill indiscriminately or excessively, and choose their targets with great care. (It is revealing that, as one informant told Nelson, the moose is the 'only animal never mentioned in their stories of the Distant Time' – a free translation of *Kk'adonts'idnee*, their body of creation legends.) The moose, Nelson notes, 'is easily the most important resource among all animal species'.[8] So the modern Koyukon language is predictably rich in terms for different types of moose:

Subsistence hunters of moose on the south fork of the Koyukuk River, Kanuti National Wildlife Refuge, Alaska.

> *dineega*   moose (blanket term)
> *k'iyeedza'*   largest type of bull moose

didaayee gida'	four-year-old bull moose
didaayee yoza	two- to three-year-old bull moose
diyozee	cow moose (blanket term)
baggoy adinee	cow moose without calves

And so on. The language is richer and more exact still in terms for the moose body parts used in cooking:

bitlee'	head
bintsiyh	nose
binogha'	eyes
bitoola'	ears

There are well over thirty such anatomical terms in all. Moose hide is almost as important to the Koyukon as moose meat: moose skin with the fur intact is used for mattresses (the stuffing is provided by a mixture of moose hair and waterfowl feathers), rawhide is used for the manufacture of sleds and snowshoes, and for all types of clothing.

Nelson notes with surprise that, notwithstanding its vital role in the local economy, the moose is accorded very little supernatural significance, and there are only a relatively small number of superstitions or ritual practices attached to moose hunting and eating. One of the few anthropologists to study the region before Nelson, Jules Jette, left a record that moose possess a spirit – *yeega* – but only in the rutting season. No trace of this belief appears to have survived. Moose are treated with a certain amount of respect: for example, those about to go on a hunt will speak in euphemisms, such as 'I will go out and try to seek a moose track'. It is not done to boast about one's hunting exploits – but that is a mode of respect that applies to all game animals, not the moose alone.

Perhaps the most curious lesson Nelson took from his time with the Koyukon was not anthropological but ethnological: moose, he learned, have a pronounced aversion to caribou, and will rapidly vacate an area when the caribou start to move in. 'A Koyukan elder explained that they dislike the noise caribou make, walking carelessly through the brush and running to and fro without reason. Moose are quiet animals, he said, and they cannot abide these clamorous intruders.'[9] Nelson's reports have been corroborated and amplified by other anthropologists of cold climates.[10]

To be sure, these cases of moose-dependent communities are as marginal to Western cultural life as they are to its economy. With the decline in importance of moose meat as a primary foodstuff, and of moose hide as a source of clothing, the creature continues to grow in symbolic significance, but now in entirely new directions: above all, into cuteness. As so often in the story of Western expansion, that which once was slaughtered without mercy eventually becomes the object of pity, piety and affection. And so, what it loses in nutritional significance, the moose more than gains in cultural and emotional terms.

THE CUTE MOOSE

The perception that moose might be cute – rather than majestic, or frightening, or ugly – is of relatively recent date: Theodore Roosevelt slaughtered alcines as well as ursines, but he left us with the Teddy Bear, not the Teddy Moose – though a glance round toy shops in Maine and other moose-rich regions might easily suggest otherwise, so overwhelmingly dense is the local population of small, plush, cuddly toys with soft antlers.

Similarly, the whole world recognizes Mickey Mouse, not Mickey Moose. It is telling that the Disney Corporation, whose

Young moose respond readily to signs of affection from humans, and in appropriate homes may even be kept as pets. Here, an employee of the US Fish and Wildlife Service in Alaska holds a small calf.

Mervyn Peake's drawing of a 'knotted-tail' moose, from *Letters from a Lost Uncle* (1948).

vast wealth is founded on anthropomorphized rodents and fowls, should have waited until 2003 to produce moose characters of any great appeal to children: Rutt (rather a bawdy name?) and Tuke, supporting characters in the animated feature *Brother Bear*. Earlier Disney ventures into moosedom are largely forgotten. *The Moose Hunt* (1931) was the first cartoon in which Mickey's dog Pluto is called by name; *Moose Hunters* (1937) featured Goofy and Donald Duck dressing up as a cow moose to lure an amorous bull.

The closest Disney ever came to creating a franchise alcine was *Morris, The Midget Moose* (1950). Morris, as the title suggests, was very small, but possessed huge antlers, and his disproportion made him an outcast and a laughing stock – for those with tender hearts, the scenes of Morris's tears are harrowing – until he teamed up with Balsam, a large moose with tiny antlers. Together, the friends took on and defeated the leader of the herd.

152

This is a Moose
(the Knotted-tail kind)

Until recently, this was just about the complete extent of Disney's investment in moose imagery, save for an interesting sideline: during World War II, artists from the Disney studios were often put to work designing emblems and patches for military units. The Royal Canadian Air Force Wireless Station at Patricia Bay, British Columbia, were given a patch that showed a Disney moose with radio signals flashing behind him. For the USAF, Disney designed at least two other moose emblems, one for the 450th Bombardment Squadron, which showed a crouching moose with boxing gloves, and one for the 3rd Air Force, which showed a flying moose with bombs in its antlers.

A few years after the abortive career of Morris the Midget Moose, in 1955, the first major moose character in an American children's television show made his debut. Mr Moose – a hand puppet – was a regular character on the popular *Captain Kangaroo* show, and for thirteen years, until 1968, countless millions of American children enjoyed watching him drop

A 'humane trophy' from the author's extensive collection of toy moose.

Canned moose.

One of the most famous children's programmes ever broadcast in the USA (though far less well known elsewhere), *Captain Kangaroo* featured a wise-cracking puppet called Mr Moose.

Bullwinkle J. Moose, the most famous moose of all time, from an episode of his adventures with the flying squirrel Rocky, first broadcast on US TV in 1959. His middle initial is, for those in on the gag, a reference to his creator, Jay Ward.

ping-pong balls on the head of Captain Kangaroo (Bob Keeshan) or telling groan-inducing knock-knock jokes. He is still recalled with affection by baby boomers.

But in the field of animated cartoons, one moose reigns supreme: Bullwinkle. Teamed up with a chipper, squeaky-voiced flying squirrel called Rocky, the *idiot savant* Bullwinkle J. Moose became an American television star for some five years, from 1959 to 1964, and his adventures can still be seen on re-runs and DVDs. In large part the creation of the producer Jay Ward and writer-actor Bill Scott, the *Bullwinkle* shows were a curious combination of relatively crude animation technique with remarkably sophisticated verbal humour. As many reviewers noted at the time of its first airings, it was really the first show of its kind to appeal in equal measure to very small children and to sharp-witted adults. Many of the storylines spoofed Cold War anxieties: the show's regular villain was the incompetent Pottsylvanian spy Boris Badenov, who, with his sultry Mata

A poster for the 2000 film version of *Rocky and Bullwinkle*, which combined live action with animation.

Hari companion Natasha, tried to overthrow the free world on a weekly basis, only to be thwarted by the moose-squirrel combo.

Four decades after the show ceased production, Bullwinkle is still an all but universally recognized character in America. His fame has recently spread to younger generations thanks to an expensive (some US$90 million) if not very appealing feature film mixing live action and computer-generated animation, *The Adventures of Rocky and Bullwinkle*, starring Robert De Niro as 'Fearless Leader' and Rene Russo as Natasha.[11] Even without this boost, though, Bullwinkle would have been a firmly established part of the American landscape: quite literally so in Los Angeles, where a massive statue of Bullwinkle, dressed in striped pyjamas, towers over Sunset Boulevard. And at the annual Thanksgiving Parade in New York City, a giant inflatable Bullwinkle has often hovered above the crowds.

Like Frankenstein's monster and a number of other immortal creations, Bullwinkle first appeared in the form of a dream.

Alex Anderson, one of Jay Ward's leading animators, had an annoying dream about attending a poker party with a large, goofy moose. 'I brought along this stupid moose who was doing card tricks. I woke up feeling embarrassed – I thought, you've been working too hard'.[12] As fans will recall, a frequent feature of the Bullwinkle series was the moose's failed attempt at such standard conjuring tricks as pulling a rabbit out of a hat. Anderson continued: 'There's something majestic about a moose. They're macho, but they have a comic aspect, with that schnozzola of theirs. There are few other animals so begging to be caricatured.'

Shortly after this dream, in 1950, Anderson drew his proto-type Bullwinkle cartoon as part of a storyboard for a series to be called *The Frostbite Falls Review*. Besides Rocky and Bullwinkle, the characters included Sylvester the Fox, Flora Fauna, Blackstone the Crow and Oski the Bear. The idea was that all of these animals hosted and starred in a show that they broadcast from their own station, somewhere in the North Woods. Bullwinkle's name was inspired by a car dealer in Oakland called Clarence Bullwinkel. His medium initial 'J' was a tribute to Jay Ward.

The Frostbite Falls Review never reached the screen, and its characters were put aside for about eight years, until Ward and his colleagues were sponsored to come up with a cartoon series for the breakfast foods division of General Mills, who had noted enviously how much their rival Kelloggs had benefited from sponsoring the cartoon series *Huckleberry Hound*. Ward made a pilot show, *Rocky and his Friends*, to show what could be done (and for a tiny US$5,000, at that); the initial recording session for Rocky was held on 11 February 1958. Everyone who saw the work was impressed, and General Mills signed the contract – albeit for such an absurdly low sum that Ward, despite his misgivings, had to hunt around outside the US for a studio that could produce the work at rock-bottom rates. Eventually, they settled on Mexico.

There were many nightmares to be lived through before *Rocky* finally aired on ABC, on 19 November 1959; but they proved worth the effort. The triumph was immediate; reviewers loved the show, and so did audiences. Right from the start, though, it became obvious that the nominal squirrel star was being upstaged by his moose pal; and Bullwinkle's popularity was soon consolidated by the introduction of a segment within the show entitled 'Bullwinkle's Corner', in which the moose of letters, Bard of Minnesota, would read out poems – poems that always had some comic twist. This segment was developed into the more wide-ranging 'Mr Know-It-All', in which Bullwinkle explained, disastrously, how to do things.

The show was renewed for 1960 and continued to be a hit. (One of its high spots was a four-part mini-series, 'The Last Angry Moose', in which Bullwinkle goes to Hollywood to become a movie star; he is given the screen name 'Crag Antler' and has to take lessons in slouching and mumbling like Marlon Brando.) By October 1960, less than a year after its launch, *Rocky* was the highest-rated show on American daytime television. ABC's competitor, NBC – at that time the most prestigious of the networks – watched with hungry eyes, and then carried out its predation. From 24 September 1961, the show would air on NBC, and in an evening prime-time spot – a recognition of that fact that adults were enjoying the show as much as their small children did.

The new NBC series was re-titled *The Bullwinkle Show*, and, once it was safely commissioned, Jay Ward went into a frenzy of promotional activities that would cement the American public's awareness of his alcine star for good. The most enduring of Ward's publicity stunts was his commissioning of the great

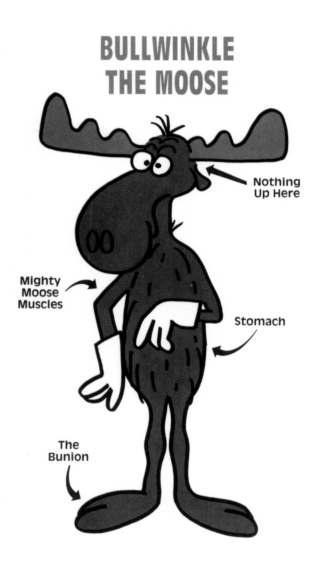

Bullwinkle statue for Sunset Boulevard. Fourteen feet (over 4 m) high, it was the work of a former art director, Bill Oberlin. The artist designed it as an obvious visual riposte to an existing statue of a Vegas cowgirl, just across the way. The grand unveiling of the statue took place on 20 September, and was accompanied by music from the 'Bullwinkle Philharmonic', an eighteen-piece orchestra. Jay Ward read a poem which spoofed Emma Lazarus's lines from the Statue of Liberty ('your huddled mooses yearning to breathe free'); Jayne Mansfield did the unveiling and the band led into the ceremonial 'Moosylvania March'. About 5,000 people attended this odd occasion, and traffic was tied up for hours.

The NBC version of Bullwinkle – which now began with a 'live action' puppet sequence of a wisecracking Bullwinkle J. Moose as host – drew even more critical raves than before, but the sailing was not smooth. NBC proved far more nervous than ABC about the show's increasingly anarchic humour, especially in the new puppet sequences, and the innovation was soon dropped. Children also seemed to grow disenchanted: the humour was now too frequently above their heads.

In 1962 Bullwinkle became the star of a newspaper comic strip, finely drawn by an artist called Al Kilgore; it ran for three years. But this was a minor event compared to Ward's most ambitious publicity stunt: the 'Moosylvania' campaign. According to the show's mythology, Bullwinkle, though a long-time resident of Frostbite Falls, was in fact a native of the horrible little place called Moosylvania. Ward put a blank cheque in the hands of one of his employees, Skip Craig, and told him to go off and buy an island somewhere in the north of Minnesota. The task proved difficult, until Craig encountered a local dentist who thought the whole idea hilarious, and rented Ward an island for three years.

Bullwinkle: an anatomical study.

Ward went into overdrive. In October 1962 he set off on a cross-country promotional tour, agitating for 'Moosylvania' to be recognized as the fifty-second state. (Ward suggested that the fifty-first state would probably turn out to be Mississippi.) Dressed up in a cod-Napoleonic uniform, and standing atop a large Ford sound-truck which blared out 'Moosylvania' songs, he created a traffic nuisance in 22 cities. At one point they even drew up outside the White House, hoping for an endorsement from President Kennedy, but more than a dozen security guards pounced on them. Ward, unperturbed, claimed diplomatic immunity. Later that day they discovered that the president's mind was on matters far graver than the fate of Moosylvania: it was the first day of the Cuban Missile Crisis.

The Moosylvanian campaign peaked on 16 November 1962 with a 'Moose's Day Parade' in Manhattan. It had been some two months in the planning, and 250 show business types took part. Fourteen gaudily decorated vehicles led a motorcade down 44th Street, flanked by 100 white-gloved policemen. The whole noisy affair culminated in a giant hot dog feast at Sardi's restaurant.

Despite these highly publicized antics, NBC was still not happy with the Bullwinkle team – especially not with their then-unheard-of habit of chomping on the hand that sponsored them. They were particularly horrified when Ward told the press that the company should change its name to the National Bullwinkle Company. NBC shifted its screening time to 5.30 p.m. on Sundays, partly as a smack on the wrist for the more irreverent of the puppet scripts. (In one of these, the Bullwinkle puppet suggested to children that they should pull the knobs off their TV sets, so as always to be tuned to the right network.) For the 1963–4 season, NBC pulled the show's slot even further back into kiddy viewing time, and scheduled it for Saturday morning. This was to be the final series.

ABC duly picked up the re-run rights in 1964, and ran the show constantly on Saturday mornings until 1973; NBC also showed some repeats in 1981–2. A decade later, the cable channel Nickelodeon began to show well-restored prints of the old series in their 'Nick at Night' service, under the title Moose-a-Rama. In 1996 General Mills re-licensed Rocky and Bullwinkle to Ted Turner's Cartoon Network. In 1991 the public service channel PBS broadcast a documentary about Bullwinkle, 'Of Moose and Men'.

Various attempts were made to bring the moose and the squirrel out of retirement. In 1976 Bill Scott wrote the script for 'Elementary, My Dear Rocky', a projected half-hour educational short in which a miniaturized Rocky and Bullwinkle go on a *Fantastic Voyage*-style trip through the human body. But the most important event of the syndication years was the release by the Walt Disney Company, starting in February 1991, of twelve commercial videos of the ABC and NBC series. Copies sold in huge numbers; the title went straight to the top of the *Billboard* video charts; celebrities from Matt Groening (who has always been prompt to admit the debt that *The Simpsons* owes to Bullwinkle), to the science fiction writer Ray Bradbury, to Steven Spielberg, all declared themselves ardent Bullwinkle fans. This proved what few had doubted: that the show's appeal was perennial. From 1995 to 1998 the Ward company (Ward himself died in 1989) worked intensively on the restoration of all the old art work and sound-tracks, so that there are now 160 half-hour shows in pristine condition. Universal TV has signed contracts with some twenty countries to the broadcast rights of a show now known as *Rocky and Bullwinkle & Friends*.

The giant shadow cast by Bullwinkle obscures all other media moose. For a short time, the animated alcine seemed to have a potential real-life competitor in the gangly form of 'Mort', who

could be seen every week in the opening credits of the well-received CBS dramatic comedy *Northern Exposure*, moseying down the main street of the fictional small town of Cicely, Alaska. Mort pauses every now and then in his wanderings to gaze with inscrutable placidity at this strange growth in the middle of his territory, then wanders away again. The effect, like the series itself, was whimsical in a highly idiosyncratic manner. Alas, the real-life Mort, a recruit from the Washington State Zoo, died not long after the sequence was shot, apparently from a condition brought on by vitamin deficiency. The series, though fondly remembered, was cancelled after five seasons.

Still, if there is no single fictional moose to rival the immortal Bullwinkle, cute and comical moose have been multiplying at a dizzying rate. In the post-Bullwinkle era, dozens and dozens of writers and cartoonists have turned to the moose as the inspiration for their children's books. One of the earliest, and probably the most famous of all, is Dr Seuss's *Thidwick the Big-Hearted Moose*; Seuss's kindly hero offers his antlers as home to his assorted woodland friends. In the 1980s a real-life romance between a bull moose and a farmer's cow drew a great deal of whimsical media attention, and was immortalized in a children's book, *A Moose for Jessica*. A complete bibliography of moose books for younger readers would occupy several pages: these include *Antlers Forever*, by Frances Bloxham and Jim Sollers; *Blue Moose* and *Return of the Moose*, by Richard D. Lansing, Jr; *Bruce Moose and the What-Ifs*, by Gary J. Oliver, H. Norman Wright and Sharon Dahl; *Deneki: An Alaskan Moose*, by William D. Berry; *Honk the Moose*, by Phil Strong; and *Latouse*

Detail from an illustration by Martin Rowson in Anna Clarke's book for children, *The Nodland Express* (1996).

My Moose, by Robert Tallon. There are now so many moose-related products on the market, especially in those parts of the United States and Canada that are rich in the species, that there are even specialist stores dedicated to mooseabilia, such as The Mangy Moose in Freeport, Maine. (Freeport is also home to a well-known L. L. Bean store, which boasts a magnificent stuffed moose.) When I visited the shop in December 2003, I found, beside countless furry moose dolls, ceramic figures, 'humane trophies' and the like, a bewildering display of moose T-shirts, sweatshirts, pyjamas, socks, caps (with and without antlers), nightshirts, mugs, plates, glasses, place-mats, book-ends, fridge magnets, key-rings, bumper stickers, postcards, playing cards, paintings, and moose products of more doubtful provenance including moose shampoo, moose soap and moose cookies. There is also, as in L. L. Bean, a full-sized adult bull moose: stuffed and not for sale. Just around the corner a shop called 'Cool as a Moose' offers rival alcine attractions.

The clientele of the Mangy Moose are also targeted as likely participants in moose-watching trips to Moosehead Lake and other local beauty spots. The scale of the moose-watching industry is considerable, though cold-hearted economists usually refer to this sort of activity by the less pretty name of 'primary nonconsumptive wildlife use'. In the year 1991, for example, America spent US$18.1 billion dollars on such wildlife pursuits, while their Canadian counterparts spent US$5.6 billion. Today, conservationists will be delighted to hear, there are many more of these 'nonconsumptive users' than hunters, trappers and anglers. And those who go on moose watches also purchase large quantities of moose photography, especially in the form of calendars, coffee table books and souvenir videos or DVDs, such as *Maine's Magnificent Moose*.

Much of this photographic work is of excellent quality – the late Bill Silliker, Jr, author of *Moose: Giant of the Northern Forest* and several other picture books, is among the most celebrated of modern moose portraitists. It must be conceded, though, that many of the painted, drawn or sculpted images of moose in modern times can only be regarded as kitsch. Andy Warhol was the proud possessor of a stuffed moose head – given to him by John Richardson – but this encounter of artist and moose is quite untypical of the modern era. To date, the one modern artist to have gained fame and honours as a moose portraitist is the Canadian painter and sculptor Charles Pachter – by chance, sometimes referred to as 'the Northern Warhol' – who won the Order of Canada for such complex images of Canadian national identity as various studies of Queen Elizabeth II riding a ceremonial moose, petting a moose or otherwise engaging with the beast. Pachter began working on his moose images in

Hundreds of individually customized moose statues were scattered around the streets and squares of Toronto for its 2000 'Moose in the City' event.

the early 1970s, but his experience of the animal dates from his childhood: a family photograph shows the artist at the age of four stroking a placid moose's head.

Somewhere between high art and unselfconscious kitsch fall the many images, often charming and entertaining, that exploit the comic potential of alcine form. In 2000, for example, 326 large sculptures of moose were distributed around the streets and squares of Toronto, each one painted or dressed up in an individual style. As Toronto's mayor Mel Lastman explained, 'We've got tourist moose, chocolate moose, dragon moose, golden moose, bride and groom moose and maple leaf moose.' (Lastman also dreamed up the project, in collaboration with a McDonald's executive, George Cohon.) Charles Pachter was one of the many artists who was commissioned to create moose, and came up with five: one Olympic Moose, and four for patrons who insisted that they wanted nothing less than a Pachter Moose.

Charles Pachter, *Queen on Moose*, 1972, acrylic and pastel on canvas. Pachter, a leading Canadian artist, has painted many images of moose; they can be seen as emblems of national identity, not least in this genially satirical image of Canada's head of state.

169

By and large, the event was successful: local businesses chipped in about CAN$2 million in all. Each moose stood about 8 feet tall, and cost about $6,500 dollars, of which only $1,000 went to the artist. At the end of the year, the sculptures were auctioned off for charity. But there were carpers: for one thing, it was widely observed, the event may have been *orignal* but it was hardly original, since Lastman had been inspired by Chicago's 1999 'Cows on Parade' displays – and Chicago had been inspired by a similar event in Zürich. Nor did everyone see the wit or beauty of the moose, especially when they were adorned with plugs for their sponsors. Nonetheless, the 'Moose in the City' project may still be regarded as one of the high water marks of alcine history.

ENVOI

It is not only the visual artists who are guilty of neglecting our quadruped. Since the age of Thoreau and Whitman, very few imaginative writers of standing have turned their attention to the moose; indeed, for such a significant feature of the American ecosystem, the moose is all but invisible in the higher ranges of the national literatures of the United States and Canada. There are one or two honourable exceptions: Anne Sexton, for example, in her sequence 'Bestiary USA', from the posthumous collection *45 Mercy Street* (1976):

> American Archangel you are going –
> your body as big as a moving van –
> the houses, the highways are turning you in.
> Before my house was, you stood there grazing
> and before that my grandfather's house with you
> on the wall . . .

John Kearney's 2002 moose sculpture made of car bumpers, Chicago, Illinois.

And Robert Duncan, who, in 'Poetry, A Natural Thing', interestingly picks up on the story of Stubbs and the Duke of Richmond's moose:

> . . . a moose painted by Stubbs,
> where last year's extravagant antlers
>   lie on the ground.
> The forlorn moosey-faced poem wears
>   new antler-buds,
>   the same,
>
> 'a little heavy, a little contrived',
>
> his only beauty, to be
>   all moose.

The last word must go to one of America's greatest twentieth-century poets, Elizabeth Bishop, whose justly famous piece 'The Moose' describes a typical nocturnal road encounter between alcine and human; or not so typical, because on this occasion a poet was there to give resonant words to the epiphany. The poem's narrator is one of the passengers on a night-time bus ride to Boston, probably southwards down the Eastern seaboard, maybe in Maine:

> . . . a moose has come out of
> the impenetrable wood
> and stands there, looms, rather,
> in the middle of the road . . .

The chance interruption of their journey inspires a 'sweet sensation of joy' in all the passengers, who are momentarily swept out of their more petty worries or ambitions and thrilled with a sense of privilege. This moose is a blessing. Why a moose? Down-to-earth answer: well, simply because it was; and Bishop was one of the passengers on that bus. More ruminative answer: perhaps because most of the other free-ranging creatures that bring to our urban minds the sense of wildness and wilderness are predators, fearful and destructive as well as admirable. But moose are herbivorous, and tend to timidity; their odd combination of potential power and habitual gentleness reminds us primarily of another large quadruped. Hence Thoreau's telling phrase 'God's own horses', which can make a kind of sense even to strict atheists.

For the travellers in 'The Moose', this nocturnal meeting is the closest most, if not all of them, will ever come to undergoing a mystical experience. For those who have read Lévi-Strauss's autobiography, *Tristes tropiques*, Bishop's poem will

Moose in an Alaskan river.

summon up memories of that strange book's magnificent, one-sentence finale, which celebrates what the anthropologist calls, in English translation, *unhitching* – the rare, invaluable experience of shedding all merely human concerns and climbing 'that tenuous arch linking us to the inaccessible'. Among Lévi-Strauss's instances of such unhitching is 'the brief glance, heavy with patience, serenity and mutual forgiveness' that one may sometimes exchange with a cat. For me, as for the bus's passengers, it was meeting an adult female moose that brought about the fleeting sense of liberation. This brief book has been, in part, a tardy thank-you letter to that adult female's species.

Timeline of the Moose

40 million years BC	20 million years BC	2 million years BC	c. 900,000 years BC	c. 250,000 years BC
The earliest known ancestors of ruminant quadrupeds are established in North America and Europe 	The first members of the deer family, *Cervidae*, appear in Eurasia	The true ancestor of the modern moose, *Libralces gallicus* or Gallic moose, evolves in the savannahs of Western Europe, spreading as far north as the British Isles	The *Libralces latifrons*, or the Broad-Fronted Moose, develops	*Libralces latifrons* crosses the so-called Bering Land Bridge from Siberia into Alaska

1556	1567	1606	1632
A detail in one of the maps published in G. B. Ramusio's *Navigationi e viaggi* shows a large antlered quadruped; this is probably the earliest European representation of a North American moose	Olaus Magnus describes the various ways in which moose have been domesticated, especially in Sweden	First English-language record of a 'Mus' by Captain Thomas Hanham (published 1625)	King Gustavus Adolphus of Sweden is shot at the battle of Lützen and dies almost at once; he had mistakenly believed that his elk-skin doublet was bullet-proof

1784	1853	1876	1883	1893
The French naturalist Buffon makes his first examination of a live moose	Thoreau and Lowell go on moose hunts in Maine	The Earl of Dunraven laments that moose are being hunted into extinction in North America	Moose hunting becomes regulated by law in Maine; other states follow the example over the next decade or so	Alexander Proctor's sculptures of moose are seen by thousands of visitors to the World's Columbia Exposition in Chicago

c. 75,000 years BC	53 BC	*c.* AD 400–600	*c.* AD 950	*c.* 1501–4
The Broad-fronted moose is now extinct; the modern moose is firmly established throughout the boreal regions of North America	In *De bello Gallico* Julius Caesar gives the earliest known written account of *alces*	European elk are retreating from western Europe into Scandinavia and Russia	Moose are now completely extinct in France, southern Germany and other southern parts of Europe, but persist in northern Germany, Poland and, for a while, in Switzerland	Albrecht Dürer paints an elk

1671	1672	1697	1721	1767
Montanus's account of moose perpetuates the legend that they can boil water in their stomachs and regurgitate the scalding fluid over predators	Denys publishes a detailed account of Native American techniques of moose hunting	Dr Thomas Molyneux publishes his speculations on the possible links between moose and the extinct Irish elk	Pierre de Charlevoix notes that the uncontrolled slaughter of moose in NorthAmerica threatens them with extinction in certain ranges	King George III is presented with a Canadian moose

1916	1955	2000	2007	2008
Samuel Merrill's classic *The Moose Book: Tales from Northern Forests* is published	Peterson's *North American Moose* is the first full-length scientific monograph devoted to the species	Toronto's Moose in the City Project: 326 large sculptures of moose, each one with a distinctive appearance, are exhibited around the town	Swedish entrepreneurs outline plans for the construction of a giant wooden moose, large enough to hold a restaurant and several galleries	Scientists establish that the antlers of bull moose act as amplifiers, greatly improving the range and quality of their hearing

References

1 THE NATURAL MOOSE

1 As this book was being completed, in March 2008, it was reported
   that American scientists had established beyond reasonable
   doubt that antlers may significantly improve the animals'
   hearing. For a lively account, see David Derbyshire, 'Amplifying
   Antlers that Help Mr Moose Hear for Miles', *Daily Mail*, 21
   March 2008.

2 THE EUROPEAN MOOSE OR ELK

1 Anne Taplin, *Memories of the Kaiser's Court* (New York, 1914),
   pp. 254–5.
2 Olaus Magnus, *De gentibus septentrionalibus* (Basel, 1567), p. 484;
   also in Samuel Merrill, *The Moose Book: Facts and Stories from
   Northern Forests* (New York, 1916; 2nd edn 1920), pp. 308–9.
3 William Jardine, *Naturalists's Library* (London, 1835).
4 Nicolas Denys, *Description geographique et historique des costes de
   L'Amérique septentrionale* (Paris, 1672), as *The Description and
   Natural History of the Coasts of North America (Acadia), 1672*, ed.
   and trans. William F. Ganong (Toronto, 1908), p. 321.
5 Edward Topsell, *The Historie of Foure-Footed Beastes* (London,
   1607); repr. as Number 561 of 'The English Experience'
   (Amsterdam, 1973), pp. 215–16.
6 Georg L. Hartig, *Lehrbuch für Jager, und für die, Welche es Werden
   Wollen* (Berlin, 1845), vol. I, p. 163.

7 Lorenz Oken, *Allgemeine Natursgeschichte dur Alle Stande* (Stuttgart, 1838), vol. VII, p. 1313.

8 Topsell, *The Historie of Foure-Footed Beastes*, pp. 211–12.

9 Richard Lyddeker, *The Great and Small Game of Europe, Western and Northern Asia and America* (London, 1901), p. 42.

10 Oken, *Allgemeine Naturgeschichte*, vol. VII, p. 1315.

11 Topsell, *The Historie of Foure-Footed Beastes*, p. 215.

12 See Merrill, *The Moose Book*, p. 273; and *Meyers Grosses Konversationslexicon* (1894; Brockhaus, 1905), under *Kunst der Naturvolker*.

13 Julius Caesar, *De bello Gallico*, 53 AD; trans. W. A. MacDevitt, with an introduction by Thomas De Quincey (New York, 2006), Book VI, chap. XXVI.

14 Pliny the Elder, *Natural History*, ed. and trans. John Bostock and H. T. Riley (London, 1855), VIII, XV, p. 263.

15 Pausanias, *Description of Greece*, ed. and trans. J. G. Frazer (London, 1919), book V, chapter XII.

16 Olaus Worm, *Museum Wormianum* (Amsterdam, 1655).

3 THE NEW WORLD MOOSE

1 See Jacques Cartier, *Narration de la navigation faite en MDXXXV et MDXXXVI par Le Capitaine Jacques Cartier aux Iles de Canada, Hochelaga, Saguenday et autres*; trans. as *Jacques Cartier and his Four Voyages to Canada* (Montreal, 1890).

2 Marc Lescarbot, *Nova Francia: A Description of Acadia, 1606*; trans. Pierre Erondelle (London, 1609); ed. H. P. Biggar (London, 1928), p. 269.

3 Brian Moore's fine novel *Black Robe* has several references to moose.

4 Ruben G. Thwaites, ed., *Jesuit Relations* (Cleveland, OH, 1896–1903), vol. XXXIX, pp. 113–15.

5 Translated by Thwaites and published in *Jesuit Relations*, vol. I, pp. 246–9.

6 Also cited in Samuel Merrill, *The Moose Book: Facts and Stories*

from Northern Forests (New York, 1916; 2nd edn 1920), pp. 12–13.

7 Modernized spelling and grammar; see also Thomas J. Lyon, ed., *This Incomperable Lande: A Book of American Nature Writing* (Boston, MA, 1989), pp. 95–7.

8 Thomas Morton, *New English Canaan* (Amsterdam, 1637), pp. 74–5. The book was not well received in Boston, and its author was imprisoned for a year.

9 Albert Franzmann and Charles Schwartz, *The Ecology and Management of the North American Moose* (Boulder, CO, 2008).

10 The 'warr' in question was against the Dutch.

11 E. E. Rich and A. M. Johnson, eds, *Hudson's Bay copy booke of letters, commissions, instructions outward, 1688–1696*, vol. XX, Hudson's Bay Record Society (1957), pp. 231, 236.

12 Paul Dudley, 'A Description of the Moose-Deer in America', *Philosophical Transactions of the Royal Society* (1721), pp. 165ff.

13 William F. Ganong, *Natural History of the Coasts of North America* (Toronto, 1908), p. 187; Randolph L. Peterson, *North American Moose* (Toronto, 1955), p. 21.

14 L. P. Kellogg, *Early Narratives of the Northwest, 1634–1699* (New York, 1917), p. 207.

15 See Peterson, *North American Moose*, p. 21; Thwaites, *Jesuit Relations*, vol. LXVII, p. 213.

16 L. P. Kellogg, *Journal of a Voyage to North America, Translated from the French of Pierre François Xavier de Charlevoix* (Chicago, 1923), vol. I, p. 182.

17 Ernest Thompson Seton, *Lives of Game Animals* (New York, 1929), p. 189.

18 Franzmann and Schwartz, *The Ecology and Management of the North American Moose*, p. 74.

19 Henry David Thoreau, *The Maine Woods* [1864] (Princeton, NJ, 1982), pp. 163–4.

20 Franzmann and Schwartz, *Ecology and Management of the North American Moose*, p. 40.

4 THE ENLIGHTENMENT MOOSE

1 Comte de Buffon (George-Louis Leclerc), *Histoire naturelle, générale et particulière*, ed. Sonnini, (Paris *l'an XI* [i.e., 1802–3 in the non-Revolutionary calendar]), vol. XXX, pp. 92, 145. See illustration.

2 Thomas Jefferson, *Notes on the State of Virginia* (London, 1787), p. 53.

3 See S. E. Ambrose, *Undaunted Courage: Meriwether Lewis, Thomas Jefferso, and the Opening of the American West* (New York, 1996).

4 All citations are from *George Stubbs, 1724–1806*, exh. cat., Tate Gallery, London (1984), pp. 118–19.

5 Thomas Bewick, *A General History of Quadrupeds* (Newcastle-upon-Tyne, 1790), pp. 120–21.

6 Charles Shain and Samuella Shain, eds, *The Maine Reader* (Boston, MA, 1991), p. 127.

7 Henry David Thoreau, *The Maine Woods* [1864] (Princeton, NJ, 1982), pp. 110–11.

8 Ibid., p. 115.

9 Ibid., pp. 119–20.

10 Henry David Thoreau, *Journals*, 23 March 1856.

5 THE SYMBOLIC MOOSE

1 George Shiras III, in an article in *National Geographic Magazine*, (May 1912), pp. 447–9.

2 I owe this point to Professor Sir Christopher Frayling, whose father worked for the HBC for many years.

3 I owe this information to Dr Glyn Johnson.

4 Personal communication with Dr Franzmann, dated 1993. Cited in Albert Franzmann and Charles Schwartz, *The Ecology and Management of the North American Moose* (Boulder, CO, 2008), p. 69.

5 Theodore Roosevelt et al., *The Deer Book* (New York, 1924), p. 209.

6 Theodore Roosevelt, in an article in *Scribner's Magazine* (February 1916).

7 Cited in Bill Silliker and Walter Griggs, *Moose-cellania: A Collection of All Things Moose* (Camden, ME, 2004), p. 86.

8 Agnes Herbert, *The Moose* (London, 1913), p. 145.

9 Ernest Thompson Seton, *Trail of an Artist-Naturalist* [1940] (London, 1951), p. 216.

10 Cited in Franzmann and Schwartz, *The Ecology and Management of the North American Moose*, p. 52.

11 Windham Wyndham-Quin, fourth Earl of Dunraven, *The Great Divide* (London, 1876), p. 27; reprinted in 1927 as *Hunting in Yellowstone*.

12 Madison Grant, 'The Vanishing Moose, and their Extermination in the Adirondacks', *Century Magazine*, XLVII (1894), pp. 345–56.

6 THE MODERN MOOSE

1 See Valerius Geist, *Deer of the World* (Shrewsbury, 1999), p. 229.

2 See Albert Franzmann and Charles Schwartz, *The Ecology and Management of the North American Moose* (Boulder, CO, 2008), p. 251. For moose and the relationship to wolves on Isle Royale, see Durward Allen, *Wolves of Minong: Their Vital Role in a Wild Community* (Boston, MA, 1979).

3 Adolph Murie, *A Naturalist in Alaska* [1961] (New York, 1963), p. 103.

4 Ibid., p. 108.

5 Geist, *Deer of the World*, p. 223.

6 Franzmann and Schwartz, *The Ecology and Management of the North American Moose*, p. 75.

7 Ibid., p. 597.

8 Richard K. Nelson, *Make Prayers to the Raven: A Koyukon View of the Northern Forest* [1983] (Chicago and London, 1986), p. 164.

9 Ibid., p. 167.

10 See, for example, the accounts of present-day Arctic hunters in Hugh Brody's work: *Maps and Dreams* (Vancouver, 1981; reprinted London, 1986), *Living Arctic: Hunters of the Canadian North* (London, 1987), etc.

11 The computer-generated Bullwinkle retains a surprising amount of his original character and charm – almost enough to redeem the film from its rather witless script and the unexpectedly poor acting by De Niro and Co.

12 Keith Scott, *The Moose that Roared: The Story of Jay Ward, Bill Scott, a Flying Squirrel and a Talking Moose* (New York, 2000), p. 21.

Bibliography

Aldrovandi, Ulisse, *Quadrupedum omnium bisulcorum historia* (Bonn, 1621)

Allen, Durward, *Wolves of Minong: Their Vital Role in a Wild Community* (Boston, MA, 1979)

Ambrose, S. E., *Undaunted Courage: Meriwether Lewis, Thomas Jefferson and the Opening of the American West* (New York, 1996)

Audubon, John James, with Revd John Bachman, *The Viviparous Quadrupeds of North America, Volume II* (New York, 1851)

Bewick, Thomas, *A General History of Quadrupeds* (Newcastle-upon-Tyne, 1790)

Bishop, Elizabeth, *The Complete Poems, 1927–1979* (New York, 1983)

Boucher, Pierre, *Histoire véritable et naturelle* (Paris, 1664)

Brody, Hugh, *Maps and Dreams* (Vancouver, 1981; reprinted London, 1986)

——, *Living Arctic: Hunters of the Canadian North* (London, 1987)

Buffon (George-Louis Leclerc, Comte de Buffon), *368 Animal Illustrations from Buffon's Natural History* (New York, 1993)

Caraman, Philip, *Norway* (London, 1969)

Cartier, Jacques, *Narration de la navigation faite en MDXXXV et MDXXXVI par Le Capitaine Jacques Cartier aux Iles de Canada, Hochlega, Saguenday et autres*, trans. as *Jacques Cartier and his Four Voyages to Canada* (Montreal, 1890)

——, *The Voyages*, ed. H. P. Biggar (New York, 1924)

Chunovic, Louis, *The Rocky and Bullwinkle Book* (New York, 1996)

——, *The Northern Exposure Book* (London, 1993)

Coady, John W., 'Moose', in *Wild Mammals of North America*, ed. Joseph A. Chapman and George A. Feldhamer (Baltimore, MD, 1982)

De Champlain, Samuel, *Les Voyages de Sieur de Champlain* (Paris, 1613)
——, *Les Voyages de la Nouvelle France Occidentale, dicte Canada* (Paris, 1632)
——, *The Voyages and Explorations, 1604–1616, Together with the Voyage of 1603*, ed. and trans. A. N. Bourne and E. G. Bourne (Toronto, 1911)

De Charlevoix, Pierre Francois Xavier, *Journal of a Voyage to North America*, ed. and trans. Louise Phelps Kellogg, (Chicago, IL, 1923)

Denys, Nicolas, *Description geographique et historique des costes de L'Amérique septentrionale* (Paris, 1672); as *The Description and Natural History of the Coasts of North America (Acadia), 1672*, ed. and trans. William F. Ganong (Toronto, 1908)

Derbyshire, David, 'Amplifying Antlers That Help Mr Moose Hear for Miles', *Daily Mail* (21 March 2008).

Diamond, Jared, *Guns, Germs and Steel: The Fates of Societies* (London, 1997)

Dreyer, J.L.E., *Tycho Brahe: A Picture of Scientific Life and Work in the Sixteenth Century* (Edinburgh, 1890)

Dudley, Paul, 'A Description of the Moose-Deer in America', *Philosophical Transactions of the Royal Society* (1721)

Duncan, Robert, *The Opening of the Field* (New York, 1973)

Egerton, Judy, et al., *George Stubbs, 1724–1806*, exh. cat., Tate Gallery, London (1984)

Eisler, Colin, *Dürer's Animals* (Washington, DC, 1991)

Elliott, R.W.V., *Runes* (Manchester, 1959)

Emerson, Hunt, with Kevin Jackson, 'Moose Lore!', in *Fortean Times* [London], no. 231 (January 2008)

Finch, Robert, and John Elder, *The Norton Book of Nature Writing* (New York, 1990)

Franzmann, Albert, and Charles Schwartz, *The Ecology and Management of the North American Moose* (Boulder, CO, 2008)

Geist, Valerius, *Deer of the World* (Shrewsbury, 1999)

Gesner, Konrad, *Historiae Animalium*, see Topsell, Edward

Gould, Steven Jay, *Ever Since Darwin: Reflections in Natural History* (New York, 1977)

Gorges, Sir Fernando, *A Brief Relation of the Discovery and Plantation of New England* (London, 1622)

Grant, Madison, 'The Vanishing Moose and their Extermination in the Adirondacks', *Century Magazine*, XLVII (1894)

Hardy, Campbell, *Sporting Adventures in the New World* (London, 1855)

Hearne, Samuel, *A Journey from Prince of Wales' Fort in Hudson's Bay to the Northern Ocean in the Years 1769, 1770, 1771 and 1772*, ed. J. B. Tyrell (Toronto, 1911)

Herbert, Agnes, *The Moose* (London, 1913)

Hornaday, W. T., *The American Natural History* (New York, 1904)

Jackson, Kevin, 'Any Which Way But Moose', *The Independent* [London], 8 February 2001.

Jefferson, Thomas, *Notes on the State of Virginia* [written 1781] (London, 1787)

Joliffe, Norm, *Bear and Moose: The Saga of Big Game Hunting in the Northeast Wilderness* (Waterville, ME, 1987)

Josselyn, John, *New Englands Rarities Discovered* (London, 1672)
——, *New England's Prospect: An Account of Two Voyages to New England* (London, 1674)

Joyce, James, *Finnegans Wake* (New York, 1939)

Julius Caesar, *De bello Gallico*, AD 53; trans. W. A. MacDevitt, with an introduction by Thomas De Quincey (Thorndike, ME, 2006)

King, Major W. Ross, *The Sportsman and Naturalist in Canada* (London, 1866)

Lescarbot, Marc, *The History of New France*, ed. and trans. W. L. Grant (Toronto, 1907–14)
——, *Nova Francia: A Description of Acadia, 1606*; trans. Pierre Erondelle (London, 1609); ed. H. P. Biggar (London, 1928)

Lowell, James Russell, 'A Moose Hunt', *Putnam's Magazine* (New York, 1853); reprinted in *The Maine Reader*, ed. Charles Shain and Samuella Shain (Boston, MA, 1991)

Lyddeker, Richard, *The Great and Small Game of Europe, Western and*

Northern Asia and America (London, 1901)

Lyon, Thomas J., *This Incomperable Lande*: *A Book of American Nature Writing* (New York, 1989)

Mackenzie, Alexander, *Voyages from Montreal, on the River St Lawrence Through the Continent of North America, to the Frozen and Pacific Oceans in the Years 1789 and 1793* (London, 1801)

Magnus, Olaus, *De gentibus septentrionalis* (Basel, 1567)

McNair, Wesley, ed., *The Quotable Moose: A Contemporary Maine Reader* (Hanover, ME, 1994)

Merrill, Samuel, *The Moose Book: Facts and Stories from Northern Forests* (New York, 1916; 2nd edn 1920)

Montanus, Arnoldus, *De Nieuwe en Onbeckende Weereld: of Beschryving van America en't Zuid-Land / The New and Unknown World; or, Description of America and the Southern Land* (Amsterdam, 1671)

Moore, Brian, *Black Robe* (London, 1985)

Morton, Thomas, *New English Canaan or New Canaan, Containing an Abstract of New England* (Amsterdam, 1632–7)

Münster, Sebastian, *Cosmographia universalis* (Basel, 1554)

Murie, Adolph, *A Naturalist in Alaska* [1961] (New York, 1963)

Nelson, Richard K., *Make Prayers to the Raven: A Koyukon View of the Northern Forest* [1983] (Chicago and London, 1986)

Oken, Lorenz, *Allgemeine Naturgeschichte fur alle Stande* (Stuttgart, 1838)

Panofsky, Erwin, *The Life and Art of Albrecht Dürer* (Princeton, NJ, 1943)

Pausanias, *Description of Greece*, ed. and trans. J. G. Frazer (London, 1919)

Pennant, Thomas, *Arctic Zoology* (London, 1785)

Peterson, Randolph L., *North American Moose* (Toronto, 1955)

Pliny the Elder, *Natural History*, ed. and trans. John Bostock and H. T. Riley (London, 1855)

Pomet, Pierre, *Histoire générale des drogues* (Paris, 1735)

Pontoppidan, Erich, *A Natural History of Norway* (London, 1755)

Ramusio, Giovanni Battista, *Navigationi e viaggi* (Rome, 1556)

Rich, E. E., and A. M. Johnson, eds, *Hudson's Bay Copy Booke of Letters, Commissions, Instructions Outward, 1688–1696* (London, 1957)

Rodgers, Art, *Moose* (Grantown-on-Spey, 2001)

Roosevelt, Theodore, et al., *The Deer Book* (New York, 1924)

Scott, Keith, *The Moose that Roared: The Story of Jay Ward, Bill Scott, a Flying Squirrel and a Talking Moose* (New York, 2000)

Seton, Ernest Thompson, *Lives of Game Animals*, 4 vols (New York, 1925–8)

——, *Trail of an Artist-Naturalist* [1940] (London, 1951)

Sexton, Anne, *45 Mercy Street* (Boston, MA, 1976)

Shain, Charles, and Samuella Shain, eds., *The Maine Reader* (Boston, MA, 1991)

Stoate, Christopher, *Taxidermy: The Revival of a Natural Art* (London, 1987)

Taplin, Anne, *Memories of the Kaiser's Court* (New York, 1914)

Thompson, David, *Narrative of His Explorations in Western America, 1784–1812*, ed. J. B. Tyrell (Toronto, 1916)

Thoreau, Henry David, *The Maine Woods* [1864] (Princeton, NJ, 1982)

Thwaites, Ruben G., ed., *Jesuit Relations and Allied Documents, 1610–1791*, 73 vols (Cleveland, OH, 1896–1903)

Topsell, Edward, *The Historie of Foure-Footed Beastes* (London, 1607); reprinted as Number 561 of 'The English Experience' (Amsterdam, 1973)

Wood, William, *New England's Prospect* (London, 1634)

Worm, Olaus, *Museum Wormianum* (Amsterdam, 1655)

Journal and Websites

ALCES — THE JOURNAL

Issued once, sometimes twice, a year. This is strictly for moose scientists, wildlife conservationists and other professionals; many of the articles are highly technical. Subscription details available from the *Alces* website.

http://bolt.lakeheadu.ca/~alceswww/alces.html

MOOSEWORLD

A large, entertaining and well-constructed site for the general reader, which includes galleries of moose photographs, moose products, and a question-and-answer service. Suitable for children.

www.mooseworld.com

ULTIMATE MOOSE

A site also suitable for children, with a strong emphasis on comedy and whimsy. Highlights include apparently exhaustive lists of appearances by (and references to) moose in films and on both British and American TV – for example, the famous stuffed moose head joke from the *Fawlty Towers* episode 'The Germans'. Includes links to several other relevant sites.

www.smouse.force9.co.uk/moose.htm

THE NORTH AMERICAN MOOSE FOUNDATION

A non-profit body concerned with conservation and education. Founded in 1981, it based in Mackay, Idaho.

www.moosefoundation.org

Acknowledgements

The bible of contemporary moose studies, which should be owned by everyone with a serious interest in the creature, is Franzmann and Schwartz's monumental *Ecology and Management of the North American Moose*, which is primarily a scientific and practical study, but with an outstanding first chapter on the species' cultural history and a colossal, admirably scholarly bibliography; I am grateful to the authors both for instruction and for inspiration. In matters of moose history, my greatest debt is to Samuel Merrill's pioneering study *The Moose Book*, long since out of print save in an unappealing print-on-demand format, but well worth seeking out from antiquarian booksellers.

It is a pleasure to record my gratitude to the artists who so generously offered their work free of charge: Pryll Barrett, Katie Cuddon, Hunt Emerson, Elizabeth Flowerday, Magnus Irvin, Simon Nicholas, Martin Rowson; and to Christopher Cox and John Kenyon for their photographs. More formal thanks are due to various librarians: the staff of Bowdoin College in Maine; Ann Sylph at the Library of the Zoological Society of London; David Weston and colleagues at Glasgow University Library; Graham Nisbet at the Hunterian Museum, Glasgow; and Dr Wallace Dailey, Curator of the Theodore Roosevelt Collection at Harvard University. Also to Simon Oxley at Merchant Ivory; Moosehead Breweries; the Purple Moose Brewery, Wales; and to the Roerich Foundation, New York. Dr Alexander Minaev of the Kostroma Moose Farm, Russia, was a prompt and courteous correspondent: I hope we will meet one day. Particular thanks to

Prof. Rolf Peterson, author of *The Wolves of Isle Royale: A Broken Balance*, and the artist Charles Pachter, whose children's book *M is for Moose* will be published shortly in Canada.

Friends and family: in addition to those already mentioned, I am in debt to John Archer, John Baxter, Alastair Brotchie, Peter Carpenter, Kathleen and Rob Flory, Christopher Frayling, Mark Godowski, Neil Hornick (especially for lending me early Disney moose cartoons), Ian Irvine, Alma and Alec Jackson, Mike Jay, Kevin Loader, Tom Lubbock, Roger and Henrietta Parsons, Mark Pilkington, Michell and Ron Royal, Jonathan Sawday, Nikolai Ssorin-Chaikov, Peter Swaab, David Thompson, Martin Wallen, Marina Warner and Lisa Williams. My sincere apologies to anyone whose name I have overlooked.

Jonathan Burt, the creator of the Animal series, made this book possible and has been a good friend throughout; Michael Leaman, who commissioned it, greeted its long and meandering route to completion with great patience. The wit, erudition and spontaneous 'pataphysical wisdom of Harry Gilonis helped make the drudgery of picture research something that could be enjoyed as well as merely endured. Hail Ubu!

As usual, this book could never have been completed, and would have been much less of a pleasure to write, without the warm support, loyalty and encouragement of Claire Preston. I hope she will forgive the dedication to Monty, which would otherwise be hers and hers alone.

Photo Acknowledgements

The author and publishers wish to express their thanks to the below sources of illustrative material and/or permission to reproduce it. (Some sources uncredited in the captions for reasons of brevity are also given below.)

Photo Alaska Department of Public Safety: p. 147; from Ulisse Aldrovandi, *Quadrupedum omnium* . . . (Bologna, 1621): p. 61; photo Leroy Anderson / US Fish and Wildlife Service: p. 20; from John James Audubon and John Bachman, *The Quadrupeds of North America* (New York, 1851): p. 106; collection of the author: pp. 18, 34, 62, 113, 119, 154; photo Kate Banish / US Fish and Wildlife Service: p. 111; reproduced by permission of the artist (Priscilla Barrett): p. 18; photo Ronald L. Bell / US Fish and Wildlife Service: p. 6; from Thomas Bewick, *A General History of Quadrupeds* (Newcastle upon Tyne, 1790): p. 104; Bolling Collection, Miami: p. 33; photo Tim Bowman / US Fish and Wildlife Service: p. 23; photo Mike Boylan / US Fish and Wildlife Service: p. 16; British Museum, London: p. 55; from Theodor de Bry, *Admiranda narratio . . . Virginiæ . . .* (Frankfurt, 1590): p. 65; from George-Louis Leclerc, Comte de Buffon, *Histoire naturelle...* (Paris, 1769): p. 95; photos Christopher Cox: pp. 13, 62, 154; collection of the artist (Katie Cuddon), reproduced courtesy of the artist: p. 140; photo Edward S. Curtis / Library of Congress, Washington, DC (Prints and Photographs Division, Edward S. Curtis Collection – LC-USZ62-123167): p. 86; from William Daniell, *Interesting Selections from Animated Nature . . .* (London, 1809), II: p. 83; courtesy of the artist (Hunt Emerson):

p. 44; photo Everett Collection / Rex Features (598624m): p. 155; from James H. Fennell, *A Natural History of British and Foreign Quadrupeds* (London, 1843): p. 38; from Leopold Joseph Fitzinger, *Wissenschaftlich-Populäre Naturgeschichte der Säugethiere . . .* (Vienna, 1860): p. 19; Glasgow University Library Department of Special Collections (Hunterian bequest): p. 102; photo Glassel / SBW Photo/Rex Features (404238b): p. 143; from Agnes Herbert, *The Moose* (London, 1913): pp. 132, 133; Houghton Library, Harvard University (Theodore Roosevelt Collection), Cambridge, MA: pp. 128, 129; Hunterian Museum and Art Gallery (University of Glasgow): p. 100 (photo © Hunterian Museum and Art Gallery); from Theo Johnson, *Wild Animals: Mammals* (s.l., 1891): p. 136 (foot); photo John Kenyon: p. 171; from Louis Armand de Lom d'Arce, Baron Lahontan, *New Voyages to North America . . .* (London, 1703): p. 66; photo Karen Laubenstein (Big Game Alaska) / US Fish and Wildlife Service: p. 17; from Marc Lescarbot, *Histoire de la Nouvelle-France . . .* (Paris, 1609): p. 68; photos Library of Congress, Washington, DC (Prints and Photographs Division): pp. 120 (LC-USZC2-2839), 125 (Frank and Frances Carpenter collection, Mrs. W. Chapin Huntington gift - LC-DIG-ppmsc-01986), 141 (LC-USZ62-73902); photo Mike Lockhart / US Fish and Wildlife Service: p. 166; from Richard Lydekker, *The Deer of All Lands . . .* (London, 1898): p. 136 (top); from Richard Lydekker, ed., *The Royal Natural History* (London and New York, 1894): pp. 24, 27; from Olaus Magnus (Olaus Månsson), *Historia de Gentibus Septentrionalibus . . .* (Rome, 1555): p. 43 (foot); photo C. W. Mathers / Library of Congress, Washington, DC (Prints and Photographs Division, Frank and Frances Carpenter collection, Mrs. W. Chapin Huntington gift – LC-DIG-ppmsc-02019): p. 43 (top); photo Robert Mauceri: p. 98; reproduced by permission of Moosehead Breweries Ltd: p. 12 (top); from Sebastian Münster, *Cosmographia universalis . . .* (Basel, 1552): p. 59; reproduced courtesy of the artist (Simon Nicholas): p. 62; from John Ogilby, *America: Being the Latest, and Most Accurate Description of the New World . . .* (London, 1671): p. 79; reproduced courtesy of the artist (Charles Pachter): p. 168; from Mervyn Peake, *Letters from a Lost Uncle* (London, 1948), reproduced by permission of the Mervyn Peake Estate: p. 153; from Thomas Pennant,

Arctic Zoology (London, 1792), I: p. 103; from Thomas Pennant, *History of Quadrupeds* (London, 1781): p. 48; photo Rolf O. Peterson: p. 28; from Pierre Pomet, *Histoire Générale des Drogues, Simples et Composées* . . . (Paris, 1735): p. 47; from Erich Pontoppidan, *The Natural History of Norway* . . . (London, 1755), II: p. 60; private collection: p. 168; reproduced by permission of Purple Moose Brewery: p. 12 (foot); photo Bill Raften / US Fish and Wildlife Service: p. 149; from Gian Battista Ramusio, *Navigationi e Viaggi* . . . (Venice, 1556), III: p. 69; courtesy the artist (Martin Rowson): p. 165; from Etienne-Geoffroy Saint-Hilaire and Frédéric Cuvier, *Histoire Naturelle des Mammifères* . . . (Paris, 1842), IV: p. 107; from Ernest Thompson Seton, *Lives of Game Animals* (London, 1928): p. 134; photo LaVerne Smith / US Fish and Wildlife Service: p. 10; Thomas Gilcrease Institute of American History and Art, Tulsa, OK: p. 71; from Edward Topsell, *Historie of Foure-footed Beastes* . . . (London, 1607): p. 50; photo Ralph Town / US Fish and Wildlife Service: p. 26; photos US Fish and Wildlife Service: pp. 29, 152, 173; from Henry van Dyke, *Days Off and Other Digressions* (London, 1907): p. 131; photos © Zoological Society of London: pp. 19, 24, 27, 38, 48, 60, 83, 95, 103, 106, 107, 136.

Index